How did it all start? Where did we come from?

The Big Bang, the beginning of life on Earth

and being human plus forty-eight creation stories from our ancestors around the world

By

Biku Ghosh

'Myths are the essential and ready tools for thinking and communicating in African (for that matter all) philosophy. Through their meaningful and communicative features, myths exhibit and enhance the coherence, stability and continuity of the society.'

Jones M. Jaja. Nigeria

Dedicated to the future generation

Contents

It was a long, long, long, long time ago.

13.8 Billion years back, from almost nothing, from a single point with a Big Bang, our Universe began. The Universe has changed dramatically and is still evolving.

Our Universe has a story - it had a beginning, a middle where we are now, and very likely an end in some very distant future.

What made the Big Bang possible? – we don't know.

Why did it happen? – we can only speculate.

What was there before the Big Bang? – we don't know that either.

What we do know the Big Bang provided all the material in the Universe today. Even space and time, as we know them, emerged from the Big Bang. After the Big Bang, space expanded rapidly, and there was time. There was also matter and energy.

But the Universe was so hot you could not tell the difference between matter and energy. Then, within the first billionth of second of the Big Bang, matter and energy separated. Energy took the forms of gravity and electromagnetism. The matter appeared in the form of electrons and quarks. Quarks soon linked, becoming protons and neutrons.

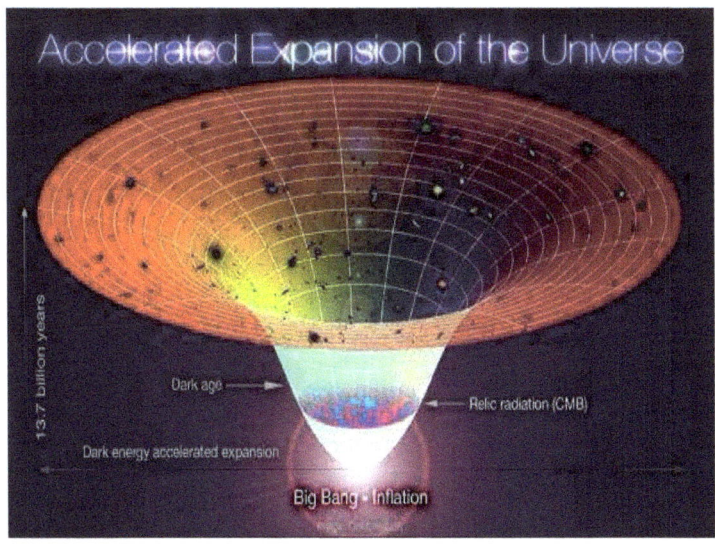

Out of the Big Bang came everything in the Universe. Imagine our Universe, everything, all the stars and galaxies that light up the night sky, our Earth and all the dark matter no one has ever seen - all of it was in a single point. So full of energy it was trillions (10^{12} - meaning 1,000,000,000,000) of degrees hot. In less than a trillionth of a second, the micro-universe expanded to nearly an octillion (10^{27}) times in size from an almost infinitely small point. Instantly, this micro-universe rushed apart way, way faster than the speed of light. From every speck of its energy jammed into a tiny dense point, it exploded with unimaginable force, propelling outward to make the billions of galaxies of our vast Universe. Also, imagine that the Big Bang did not expand through anything. That's because there was no space to expand through at the beginning of time. The Big Bang created and stretched space itself, expanding the Universe. And it is still growing!

Galaxies with stars and planets are formed

Stars and planets we see today are made up of atoms of elements like hydrogen and silicon. But the Universe back then was too hot for anything other than the most fundamental particles like quarks and photons. But as the Universe quickly expanded, the energy of the Big Bang became more and more "diluted" in space, causing the Universe to cool. Like popping open a fizzy cold drink bottle when the gas, once confined in the bottle, spreads into the air, and the temperature of the drink drops.

Rapid cooling allowed for matter as we know it to form in the Universe. About one ten-thousandth of a second after the Big Bang, protons and neutrons formed. Within a few minutes, these particles stuck together to form atomic nuclei, mostly hydrogen and helium. hundreds of thousands of years later, electrons attached to the nuclei to make complete atoms. About a billion years after the Big Bang, gravity caused these atoms to gather in vast gas clouds, forming collections of stars known as galaxies.

Where did planets like our Earth come from?

Over billions of years, stars "cook" hydrogen and helium atoms in their hot cores to make heavier elements like carbon and oxygen. Giant stars explode over time, blasting these elements into space. This matter condenses into the stars, planets, and satellites that make up solar systems like ours.

How do we know the Big Bang happened?

Observations by the scientists, looking at light beamed out by distant galaxies, have shown that the galaxies are rapidly moving away from our own galaxy, the Milky Way. An explosion like the Big Bang, which sent matter flying outward from a point, only can explain this observation.

An even more difficult question now is what was there just before the Big Bang?   The honest answer so far is that we really don't know. But there are many ideas.

Did our universe bubble out of an older one? Or is there an endless progression of blowing up bubbles, each becoming a universe? Then, each of these gave birth to even more booming bubbles in an immeasurable *multiverse*? ***So-called chaotic inflation theory.***

Or is it the Big Bounce? Long ago, philosophers in India taught that the Universe goes through an endless cycle of creation and destruction. It evolves from nothing into the complex reality we see around us before destroying itself and starting anew. Modern scientists also believe that instead of a Big Bang, the Universe expands and contracts in a cycle, bouncing back each time it shrinks to a certain size. Then, the cycle begins again.

What about dark matter? We know that dark matter makes up over 80% of all the matter in the Universe. But we really don't know much about it. When did it appear, and how? We don't know.

What is the fate of our Universe?

Will the expansion of the Universe, set in action by the Big Bang, continue forever? Or will gravity stop the growth and eventually cause all the matter in the Universe to contract in a Big Crunch? At present, no one knows for sure.

Our solar system and the Sun are born

After the Big bang, our solar system formed about 4.5 billion years ago from a dense cloud of interstellar gas and dust. The cloud collapsed, possibly due to the shockwave of a nearby exploding star, a supernova. When this dust cloud collapsed, it formed a solar nebula—a spinning, swirling disk of material. At the centre, gravity pulled more and more substances in. Eventually, the pressure in the core was so great that hydrogen atoms began to combine and form helium, releasing a tremendous amount of energy. With that, our Sun was born, eventually collecting more than 99% of the available matter in the solar system.

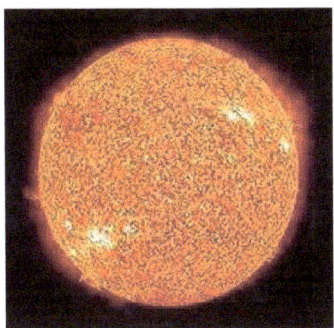

Our planets, including our Earth, are born

Matter farther out in the disk was also clumping together. These clumps smashed into one another, forming larger and larger objects. Some of them grew big enough for their gravity to shape them into spheres, becoming planets, including our own Earth, dwarf planets and large moons. And pieces of the early solar system that could never quite come together into becoming a planet, the leftovers, became asteroids, comets, meteoroids, and small, irregular moons.

So, when did life begin on our Earth?

Earth is sometimes called the *Goldilock planet*. Everything was '*just right'* for life to start here - possibly the only one in our solar system. All we know for sure from the oldest confirmed fossils of single-cell organisms is that after Earth formed, life happened on it 3.5 billion years ago. Organic molecules can be found throughout the Universe. A meteorite that fell to Earth in 1969 contained 92 different amino acids, most never seen on Earth. Could life have been seeded from elsewhere? Or maybe it was just the chance sloshing together of molecules that were bound to happen somewhere.

What made us us?

We don't know the exact answer, and the origin of life remains one of the greatest mysteries in all of science. It's likely that when Earth was young, the oceans were filled with simple chemicals essential for life. These eventually self-assembled into simple living cells. Then, it was only unicellular prokaryotes with floating DNA, no nucleus and no mitochondria. Complex eukaryoticcells with linear DNA within a nucleus and a personal power plant – mitochondria, came 2 Billion years back.

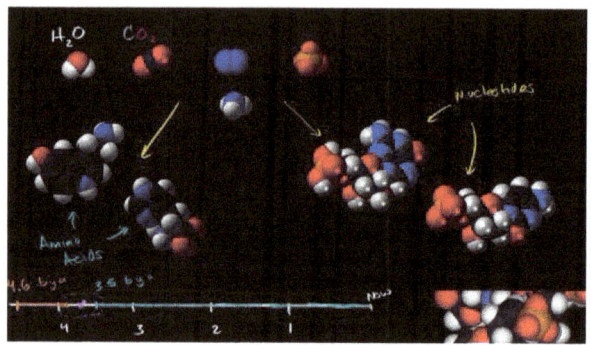

Life begins from simple molecules

3.5 billion years old Stromatolite fossil found in Australia

This started a whole new era for life on Earth. About 670 million years ago (MYA), it evolved into multicellular organisms. <u>Sponges</u> were among the earliest animals. Chemical compounds from sponges are preserved in rocks as old as 700 MYA. Then, about 580 MYA, other organisms multiplied. These varied seafloor creatures - with bodies shaped like fronds, ribbons, and even quilts - lived alongside sponges for 80 million years. Oxygen levels rose, sufficient to sustain oxygen-based life.

Turritopsis dohrnii jellyfish has no brain and heart and is probably the only immortal creature on Earth. They do not die of old age. They live up to a certain age, and then they begin to get younger and return to their initial stage and develop again. Such jellyfish only die due to predators or diseases.

But, about 541 MYA, most of the creatures disappeared, signalling a significant change in the environment still we do not understand. As environmental conditions got worse for some animals, they got better for others, bringing in a change-over in species.

The Cambrian Period (541-485 MYA) witnessed a wild explosion of new life forms. Hard body parts like shells and spines came along. Hard body parts allowed animals to drastically engineer their environments, such as digging burrows. A shift also occurred towards more active animals, with defined heads and tails for steering movement to chase prey.

Unique feeding styles partitioned the environment, making room for more varied life forms, including odd-looking organisms in evolutionary experiments, such as the five eyed Opabinia. Some groups, such as the trilobites, thrived and dominated Earth for hundreds of millions of years but eventually became extinct. The hard corals, today's dominant reef-builders, did not emerge until a couple hundred million years later.

Despite all the changes to come, nearly all current animal types were established by the end of the Cambrian period.

Life flourished on Earth with the first vertebrates (simple fishes) 490 MYA, the amphibians 350 MYA and reptiles 310 MYA. First mammals evolved 200 MYA to be followed by the non-human primates 60 MYA. The earliest apes came about 25 MYA. Gorillas evolved *8 – 6 MYA*. Later, chimp and human lineages diverged.

5.8 MYA - Orrorin tugenensis, the oldest human ancestor, could walk using two hind legs. *5.5 MYA* Forest-dwelling Ardipithecus, early "proto-human", sharing traits with chimps and gorillas came. Australopithecines appeared *4 MYA* with brains no bigger than chimpanzee's (around 400 – 500 cm^3) but could walk upright on two legs (the modern human brain is 1130 cm^3 - 1260 cm^3). These first human ancestors lived in the savannah.

3.2 MYA - Lucy, a famous specimen of *Australopithecus afarensis*, lived in Ethiopia. *2.5 MYA* - *Homo habilis* appeared, with face protruding less than earlier hominids but still retaining many ape features. Had a brain volume of around 600 cm^3.

Hominids started using stone tools regularly, created by splitting pebbles – beginning a tradition of toolmaking, which lasted a million years. Some hominids developed meat-rich diets - the extra energy from this may have led to the evolution of larger brains. *2 MYA* - Evidence of *Homo ergaster* in Africa, with a brain volume of up to 850 cm^3.

1.8 – 1.5 MYA - *Homo erectus* is found in Asia. First true hunter-gatherer ancestor, and first to have migrated out of Africa in large numbers. It attained a brain size of around 1000 cm^3. *1.6 MYA* - Possible first sporadic use of fire (suggested by sediments found in Kenya). Complex and, most notably, bifacial stone tools (hand axes and cleavers) were made and became the dominant technology until 100,000 years ago (YA).

500,000 YA - Earliest evidence of purpose-built shelters like wooden huts (found in Japan). *400,000 YA* - Early humans begin to hunt with spears. *325,000 YA* - Oldest surviving early human footprints found on the slopes of a volcano in Italy.

Very recently, on a 4,000m high Tibetan Plateau at Quesang, 200,000 years old fossiled footprints of two 7-12 years old hominid children (likely to be Denisovans or *Homo erectus)* have been discovered.

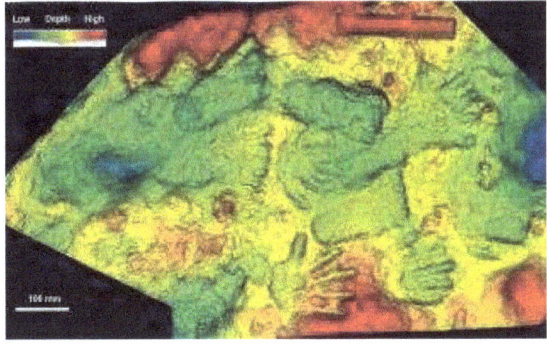

280,000 YA – Humans made the first complex stone blades and grinding stones. *230,000 YA* - Neanderthals appear and are found across Europe (but they became extinct with the advent of modern humans *28,000 YA).*

195,000 YA - <u>Our own species, *Homo sapiens*</u> (average brain volume 1350 cm$^{3)}$), appears on the scene – and shortly afterwards begins to migrate out of Africa across Asia and Europe. The oldest modern human remains of two skulls found in Ethiopia dated to this period.

| Austra-lopithecus (Hominid) | Homo Habilis | Homo Erectus | Homo Neander-thalensis | Homo Sapiens Sapiens |

Skulls of ancestors of modern humans (left to right - Australopithecus Africanus, Homo habilis, Homo erectus, Homo Sapiens)

170,000 YA – Mother of all humans Mitochondrial Eve. She is defined as the woman from whom all living humans descended in an unbroken line. There is one DNA that a human child inherits from the mother, the direct ancestor to all living people today, most likely have been living in Africa.

150,000 YA - Humans possibly capable of <u>speech</u> (not only making vocal sounds). *140,000 YA* -First evidence of long-distance trade. *110,000 YA* - Earliest beads and jewellery were made from ostrich eggshells.

50,000 YA - Great leap forward: They developed a capacity for language, and the human culture started to change rapidly. People begin burying their dead ritually; make clothes from animal hides; and develop complex hunting techniques, such as animal traps.

33,000 YA -. *Homo erectus* dies out in Asia – replaced by modern man. *18,000 YA* - *Homo Floresiensis*, "Hobbit" people, found on the Indonesian island of Flores. Only over 1 metre tall, with brains similar size to chimpanzees, yet they used advanced stone tools. *10,000 YA* - Agriculture develops and spreads. First villages. Possible domestication of dogs.

5,500 YA - Stone Age ends, and Bronze Age begins. Humans begin to smelt and work copper and tin and use them in place of stone stools. *5,000 YA* - Earliest known writing. *4,000 to 3,500 BC* - The Sumerians of Mesopotamia develop the world's first civilisation.

Becoming Human

By the early 20th century, the world's leading scientists thought Humans evolved somewhere in Europe or Asia. Neanderthals had already been found in Europe; Java Man (now known as *Homo erectus*) had been discovered in Indonesia.

Taung child: In 1924, a 2.8 MYA old fossil discovery in South Africa revolutionised the study of human evolution. In *Taung, South Africa. Rocks* blasted from a limestone quarry were brought to Raymond Dart. Digging into them, Dart remarkably found the fossilised mould of a brain. The shape and folds on the brain's surface implied it belonged to an ancient human ancestor. Further digging led Dart to another rock that the brain fit perfectly into. The creature's baby teeth revealed it was a child (probably 5-7 years old). Other features of the so-called Taung Child confirmed it was from a human ancestor.

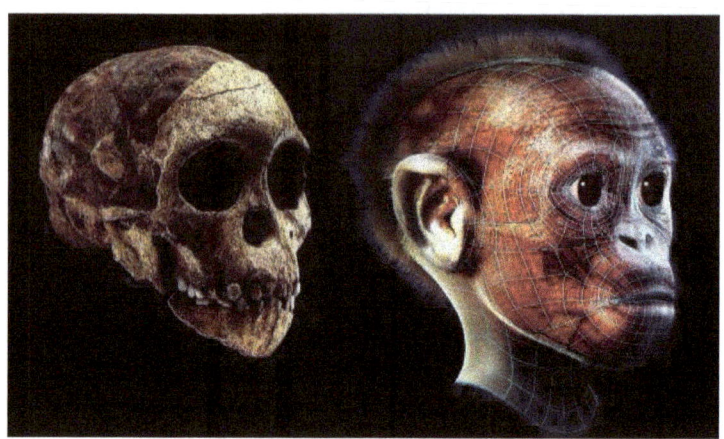

Taung child

The face lacked a pronounced brow ridge, as seen in chimps and gorillas. Its foramen magnum, a hole in the skull, where the spinal cord is continuous with the brain, was beneath the cranium. So, the creature must have stood upright, an indication of moving on two feet. Animals that travel on four legs, such as chimps and gorillas, have a foramen magnum more toward the back of the skull. It was later named as *Australopithecus africanus* species.

Scientists in the early 20th century thought that big brains made hominids unique. Until then, the only known hominid fossils were brainy species –

Neanderthals and *Homo erectus,* who clearly resembled modern humans
(Homo Sapiens).

Lucy: This view changed in 1974 with the finding in Afar, Ethiopia of Lucy,
a 3.2 million-year-old fossil of a skeleton. Lucy was only 1.1 m tall and
weighed 29 kg, and after reconstruction, looked somewhat like
a chimpanzee with a small brain.

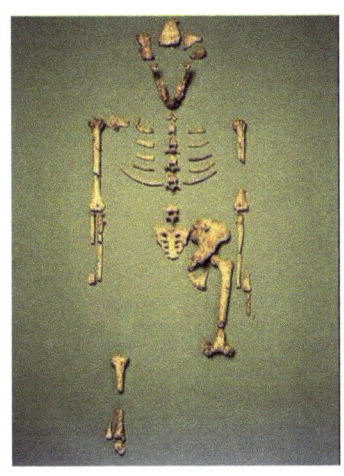

But although Lucy (Australopithecus afarensis) was small, she had the anatomy
of a biped. She had a broad pelvis and thigh bones angling toward the knees
bringing the feet in line with the body's centre of gravity and giving stability while
walking. This combination changed the view of human evolution that walking on
two feet preceded the increase in brain size.

Then in 1978, a 27-meter long trail of 3.6 million years old preserved
footprints in the Ngorongoro crater in Tanzania was found. These footprints,

left on volcanic ashes of the crater were by two bipedal (walking on two feet) creatures, walking on a humid layer that later got cemented. These are the earliest impressions from two ape-like early human ancestors, likely *Australopithecus afarensis,* and are the earliest set of bipedal footprints ever discovered. Bipedalism separated the first hominids from the rest of the four-legged apes.

Ardi: In 1994, a 4.4 million-year-old skeleton fossil was discovered at Aramis in the Afar region of Ethiopia. It was later named Ardi (Ardipithecus ramidus) and thought to be an early human-like female.

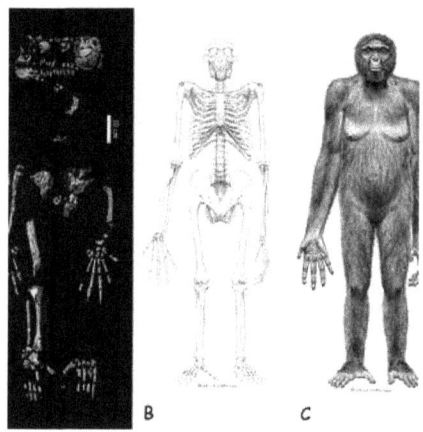

B   C

It is the most complete early hominid specimen found, with most of the skull, teeth, pelvis, hands and feet, and most extensive evidence for bipedalism.

Although the earliest hominids were capable of upright walking, they probably didn't get around precisely as we do today. They retained primitive features such as long, curved fingers and toes, longer arms and shorter legs, suggesting they spent time in trees. It was not until the emergence of *Homo erectus* 1.89 MYA that hominids grew tall, evolved long legs, shorter arms, and upright posture. They lived entirely on the grounds.

H. Erectus is the oldest known species to have a human-like body and is the longest-lived of all human species. It is agreed now that the species evolved in Africa, and soon expanded out of Africa into western Asia, then to eastern Asia and Indonesia. When and why *H. Erectus* disappeared is not known, and we don't know whether *H. Erectus* ever reached Europe. *H. Erectus* was the first human species to make hand axes, sophisticated stone tools crafted on two sides. These were probably used to butcher meat, among other purposes. Before that, the tools of ancient humans were much more primitive - simply rock flakes knapped to a sharp edge.

Turkana Boy: Scientists now agree by studying the remains of the skeleton known as Turkana Boy, *H. Erectus* walked and ran in much the same way we do. Turkana Boy, the name given to a fossil of Homo Erectus found near Lake Turkana in Kenya, is a nearly complete skeleton of a youth who lived 1.5 - 1.6 MYA.

Did *Homo erectus* use fire?

The use of fire is a significant milestone in human evolution, granting access to light, warmth, protection from predators and the ability to cook food - each of which aided survival. Scientists don't know when humans were first able to make fire at will. Early humans probably captured natural fires and kept them alight for as long as they could.

Homo Erectus may have been the earliest human relative to have controlled fire. Evidence was found of ash in a one-million-year-old sediment layer in a Cave in South Africa. It was too far inside a cave for the ash to have been caused by a lightning strike, and the spontaneous combustion of bat guano was ruled out.

Out of Africa

Us, all modern humans, are a species called Homo Sapiens. We come from Hominids, which includes all modern and extinct Great Apes (modern humans, chimpanzees, gorillas, orang-utans, and other immediate ancestors). Hominids are the largest primates, with robust bodies, well-developed forearms and no tails. Unlike other primates, they shared the ability to walk upright on two legs. Hominids diverged from other primates somewhere between 2.5 and 4 MYA in eastern and southern Africa.

Homo Sapiens, the first modern humans, evolved from their early hominid predecessors between 200,000 and 300,000 YA. Within Africa, Homo Sapiens dispersed within the whole continent soon after. Fossil studies show that between 125,000 and 75,000 YA, Homo Sapiens travelled out of Africa at least four times and reached Asia and Europe. These earlier migrations appear not to have survived, and Homo Sapiens were not invincible.

A **supervolcanic eruption at Toba** in Sumatra, Indonesia, around 75,000 YA, is one of the Earth's largest known explosive eruptions for millions of years. Toba's eruption deposited a thick layer of ash over the whole of South Asia, across India and the seas around the continent. The blast was so massive that its ashes reached Lake Malawi in East Africa at a 7300km distance. Toba eruption caused a global volcanic winter of 6-10 years and possibly a 1,000 year-long cooling episode.

It possibly affected the human evolution timeline. Scientists think that the Toba eruption may have resulted in a severe reduction in the size of the total modern human population due to its effects on the global climate. The human population may have sharply decreased to only about 10,000 surviving individuals.

Genetic evidence suggests that today's humans are descended from a very small population of between 1,000 and 10,000 breeding pairs that existed about 70,000 years ago.

But the humans living in East Africa who survived the Toba event were a new and better version of Homo Sapiens. They were soon able to leave Africa and spread to every habitable continent on Earth relatively quickly. Pushing the Neanderthals and all other remaining hominid species gradually to extinction. No trace of any modern human population has been found that might have grown outside of Africa earlier than 65,000 YA.

It is now agreed anatomically modern humans migrated again from East Africa roughly between 70,000–50,000 YA, spreading along the southern coast of Asia, then to Oceania (so-called southern route). They reached the Australian continent in canoes from southeast Asia sometime between 65,000 - 35,000 YA. Outside Africa, Australia has one of the longest histories of continuous human occupation.

The first modern humans most likely arrived in Egypt via the northern route out of Africa around 55,000 YA. From there, they spread across to the Middle East and then to Europe about 40,000 YA. Near the end of the Ice Age, over 17,000 YA humans crossed the land bridge that connected Asia and North America. They then migrated to Central and then to South America.

Over 40,000 YA, we shared the planet with subspecies of archaic human groups such as Neanderthals, Denisovans, Homo Floresiensis (Hobbits) and possibly the last remnants of Homo erectus. Though there were once many kinds of hominids, only the Homo Sapiens survived.

Others became extinct, most likely due to the combined reasons of assimilation into the modern human genome (bred into extinction), major climatic change and diseases. They were entirely replaced by early modern humans who now carry a small percentage of their DNAs.

Modern humans are the only known species to have successfully populated, adapted to, and significantly altered all seven continents, resulting in profound environmental impacts.

Why did humans move out of Africa?

As environmental changes caused the forest regions to shrink and the size of the savannah (tropical grasslands without a close canopy of trees) expanded, the early tree-dwelling hominids were likely pushed out of their homes. Hominids evolved and developed unique characteristics. Their brain size increased, and approximately 2.3 MYA, a hominid species known as Homo habilis, began to make and use simple tools. By a million years ago, some hominid species, particularly Homo erectus, began to migrate out of Africa and into Eurasia, where they started to make other advances like controlling fire.

No one is sure of the exact reasons humans first migrated off the African continent. But most likely, humans moved on in search of better living conditions: food, space and relative safety after new births swelled their numbers. The development of language around 50,000 YA allowed humans to make plans, solve problems, and organise effectively to assess the risk of leaving to find a new route out of Africa.

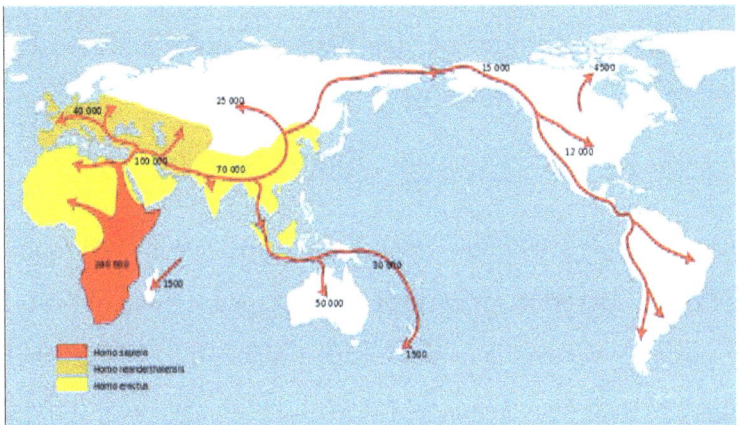

Timeline of human migration out of Africa to other continents

The successful human journey out of Africa was also possible due to falling sea levels when humans crossed into Arabia via the Bab-el-Mandeb Strait on the Red Sea. The onset of the ice age would have meant that the gap between the continents was only about 8 miles, which they somehow managed to cross.

When humans migrated from Africa to colder climates, they learnt to make clothing out of animal skins and fires to keep themselves warm. They made sophisticated weapons, such as spears and bows and arrows, allowing them to kill large animals. Humans also started using to make semi-permanent settlements, shifting from nomadic lifestyles to fixed homes. This, in turn, gave rise to established communities and the development of agricultural practices.

Now time for some old stories from around our world

Africa

Africa is the birthplace of all human species. Within Africa, Homo Sapiens dispersed around the time of its speciation, between 200,000 and 300,000 YA.

Kaang people

Kaang people are hunter-gatherers and now live in and around the area of the Kalahari Desert in Africa. Experts think they are one of the oldest peoples in the world. They have no names for themselves; they just call themselves "the People" in their own language. These bushmen have long storytelling traditions and, like many cultures, use the tales of the gods to teach about what is good and moral behaviour.

Kaang creation story

Long, long, long ago, all the animals and human beings lived together under the grounds of the world in peace with the great God Kaang, the creator of all things. Every creature understood every other. Although there was no sun, it was light and warm, and all lived in comfort and harmony.

During this happy time, Kaang began to plan the world above where all creatures would eventually live. First, he created a magnificent tree, the branches of which spread over the Earth's entire surface. He then made all the wonders within it. When he was satisfied that all was good, he dug a hole deep down where the humans and animals lived.

He took a man by the hand and led him up through the long passageway to the world above. He sat the first man down by the hole, and they waited. Soon a woman wandered up through the hole, and the couple explored their new world with all the wonders in it.

Delighted with everything, they called down the passageway. Soon, the other people and the animals, led by the curious, long-necked giraffe, were streaming out of the hole. It was magical for them. The excited birds flew up high into the tree, twittering their delight at all they could see in the sunlight. Many animals jumped and scrambled into the branches wanting to see further for themselves.

The great God Kaang, pleased at their delight with his creation, called all people and animals together under the tree. "I will tell you the laws of this new world," he said. "You are to live together in peace and harmony. You will talk together and listen to each other. But this is a new world and very fragile."

Turning to the humans, he said, "Under no circumstances must you make fire. To do so would bring great evil upon this beautiful world."

They promised solemnly that they would never do this. Satisfied, Kaang left them to enjoy their new world and went away to watch in secret. For a while, all went well.

But then the Sun started to slowly sink beneath the horizon. All the people and animals gathered together to watch this strange yet magical sight. But once the Sun had gone, the world became dark and cold.

The humans could not see as they lacked the eyesight of the animals. They became cold as they lacked the fur and feathers of the other creatures. The humans became scared. They huddled together to keep warm and shared their worries with each other. "What is happening? Will the Sun ever return?" The fear spread fast amongst them.

The animals, too, began to be afraid as they saw the people change and heard what they were saying. As the dark time continued, the fear began to turn to panic. "We are going to freeze to death. How can we live if we cannot see?" said one man. And soon, another man shouted, "We must start a fire, then we will have light and warmth, and we can survive."

"Yes, yes!" all the people agreed, forgetting the words of Kaang and their promise to him. The fire was lit, and the humans gathered around.

They could see each other in its light and could feel the warmth of the flames on their chilled bodies. They started to relax and smile at each other. The humans turned to their friends, the animals, only to find that they had begun to run away, terrified of the fire.

"Come back, there is nothing to fear." The people stood and shouted, but the animals could no longer understand them and only heard shouts and yells. This *terrified them further. In no time at all, every creature had run away and hidden.*

Sadly, the humans now remembered their promise to Kaang. They realised that by breaking it, they had also broken the understanding between humans and animals forever.

An eland has immense spiritual significance for the Kaang people

Kaang people have a deep respect for all life and think all living things, humans, animals, and plants, are connected. They believe that everything taken from nature must meet a need and should be no more than is required for the community. Amongst them, men and women's status are equal. Children are very important to them, and they get plenty of time to play and learn.

The Bushmen of Africa believe that plants and animals, rain, thunder, the wind, spring, etc., are alive. They say what we see is only the outside form or body. Inside is a living spirit that we cannot see. These spirits can fly out of one body into another. For example, a woman's spirit might sometimes fly into a leopard; or a man's spirit flies into a lion's body.

Nyamwezi people

Nyamwezi or Wanyamwezi, one of East Africa's Bantu people, are the second-largest ethnic group in Tanzania. The Swahili term Nyamwezi translates as "people of the moon".

Nyamwezi creation story

First, God created tortoises, humans and stones.

Then God made males and females of each of these, but they were told they could not have children. When they got old, they became young again.

But after a while, the pairs all wanted children.

First, the tortoises wanted children and asked. God said, but with the children will come death. But the tortoises insisted. They had children, and then death began for them.

Despite this, the human also asked repeatedly to have children. God gave in, and the humans had children, and deaths came to them as well.

The stones watched this and did not ask for children. They had neither children nor death.

Nyamwezi cultural dance

Maasai people

Maasai people nowadays live around Kenya and northern Tanzania near the game parks of the African Great Lakes. With their distinctive customs and red dress, Maasai are famous for their fearsome reputations as warriors and cattle-rustlers. Throughout the tribe's 2,000-year history, its warriors hunted lions to defend their livestock and as part of a "coming of age" ritual.

In the Maasai religion, there are two great deities. Enkai, the supreme being and creator, is the guardian over rain, the Sun, fertility, and love. Enkai is a single deity with a dual nature: benevolent Enkai Narok (Black God) and vengeful Enkai Nanyokie (Red God). Enkai Nanyokie brings famine and hunger and is found in lightning and drought.

Maasai creation story

In the beginning, there was Enkai, the God. Enkai created Naiteru-Kop, the first man, and a woman partner and sent them to Earth with herds of cattle, goats and sheep to begin a new life.

Naiteru-Kop and his partner found Earth beautiful. Abundant in natural resources--rivers, lakes, oceans, minerals, forests, plains and wildlife. They were given control over all these resources after they agreed to be good custodians and hold all creation in trust for coming generations. If they failed to keep this promise, they would bear the full consequences of their irresponsible actions.

Over time Naiteru-Kop and his partner had three sons and three daughters. The first son grew up and was given a bow and arrow so he could find his livelihood from hunting - he became a hunter. The second son received a hoe and became a farmer. The third son (father's favourite) was given a rod to herd his father's cattle once he inherited them.

The Origin of Death:

At that time, there was no death. This was how death came into the world.

There was once a man known as Leeyio who was the first man that Naiteru-kop brought to Earth. Naiteru-Kop called Leeyio and said to him: "When a man dies, and you dispose of the corpse, you must remember to say, 'man die and come back again, moon die, and stay away'.

Many months went by before anyone died. When, much later, a

neighbour's child died, Leeyio was called to dispose of the body. When he took the corpse outside, by mistake, he said: "Moon die and come back again, man die and stay away."

So, after that, no man came back from death, and the Moon came back repeatedly. A few more months passed, and Leeyio's own child died. He took the corpse outside, and this time said: "Moon die and stay away, man die and come back again."

On hearing this, Naiteru-kop said to Leeyio: "You are too late now for, through your own mistake, death was born the day when your neighbour's child died."

So that is how death came about. That is why, until today, when a man dies, he does not return, but when the Moon dies, it always comes back again.

Maasai people believe themselves to be the immediate descendent of Naiteru-Kop's last son. These great warrior people roam the endless plains

of southern Kenya and northern Tanzania in Eastern Africa. This story is taught and passed on by Maasai from generation to generation. The Enkai story explains the Maasai's reverence for nature and their spiritual attachment to livestock as a source of food and wealth.

Maasai dance

Boshongo Bantu Kuba people

This creation myth comes from the Boshongo Bantu Kuba people of Central Africa in the Democratic Republic of the Congo.

The God Mbombo Bumba

In the beginning, there was Bumba, the creator, and only darkness and water.

Bumba, a giant, white-coloured figure, had been ill for millions of years. The reason for his illness was his incurable loneliness. One day Bumba felt an intense pain in his stomach. After a while, Bumba vomited, and the Sun came out of the vomit. He continued to vomit, and next, the Moon came out, followed by the star. and they brightened the night.

The Sun's intense heat and light evaporated the water, which formed clouds in the sky. The drying continued, and after a while, hills emerged from the water and then, the sandbanks and the reefs.

Bumba puked again, and this time he vomited many animals. He brought up in his vomit the first creatures; Koy Bumba, the leopard; Pongo Bumba, a crested eagle; Ganda Bumba, a crocodile; Yo, the little fish; Kono Bumba, the tortoise; Tsetse, the lightning speed black leopard; Nyanyi Bumba, the white heron; one beetle and finally Budi, the goat. The nine animals went on to create many of the world's other creatures.

Bumba had three sons. They said they would finish creating the world. The first to try, Nyonye Ngana, vomited white ants. But he died after this. In his honour, the ants went deep in the Earth for dark soil to bury him and transformed the Earth's surface from barren sands to fertile lands. The second son, Chonganda, created a seed plant, which spread its seeds all over. That's where all the trees, grasses and flowering plants came from.

And Chedi Bumba, the third son, failed to create anything except for one bird, the last bird, the kite. Then the Universe was finished.

Tsetse, the black leopard creature, could move at lightning speed. And despite Bumba's warnings, she just couldn't stop zooming around, setting fire to things. No one could stop her, so Bumba finally banished her to the sky. She became the Goddess of Lightning, but she took away the fire with her as a last naughty act. Everyone on Earth feared her lightning strikes. The people on Earth had to live without fires which meant they had to eat raw meat and couldn't make good tools. Bumba felt sorry for them and showed them how to make fire from the woods.

Once creation was complete and peaceful, Bumba retreated into the heaves, leaving Loko Yima to serve as 'god upon the earth". The woman of the waters Nchinge lived in the East, and her son Woto became the first king of the Kuba people.

Egypt

Humans inhabited the Nile valley and its nearby deserts as environmental conditions allowed. The Lower Paleolithic period (302,000–92,000 years ago) is the earliest occupation by hominids known
in Egypt. These ancestors of modern humans often used a bifacial tool we call the Acheulian hand axe.

Acheulian hand axe

The first modern humans most likely arrived in Egypt via the northern route out of Africa around 55,000 years ago, before spreading across the Middle East and then to Europe.

Book of the dead

Egyptian mythology

The *Book of the Dead* describes how the world was created by Atum, the centre of the Egyptian sun-god.

The Universe emerged from a vast cosmic ocean of nothingness called Nun. Nun represented four principles: invisibility, infinite water, lack of direction, and darkness. Atum, the creator-sun God, created himself from nothing as a mythical Bennu bird (like a heron) by uttering his own name. For countless aeons, Atum had drifted asleep in this primordial sea called Nun. Eventually, Atum woke up and willed a small island out of the cosmic ocean.

He created Shu (the air) and Tefnut (moisture). The twins also symbolise two universal principles of human existence: life and justice. The twins separated the sky from the waters. They had children named Geb (the Earth) and Nut (the sky). Geb and Nut had four children: Seth, the God of disorder; Osiris, the God of order; and their sisters, Nephthys and Isis. This group of nine creators of the world was called the Ennead.

Atum was also known as Re, meaning the Sun at its first rising. Re ruled over the Earth, where humans and gods coexisted. Humans were created from the Eye of Re (wedjat - eye of wholeness). This happened when the eye separated from Re and failed to return. Shu and Tefnut went to fetch it, but the eye resisted. In the ensuing struggle, the eye shed tears from which humans were born. Re ruled over the Earth, where humans and gods coexisted.

The eye motif is an enduring symbol for the creator, Atum / Re. It represents the power to see, to illuminate and to act. The act of bringing the eye back to the creator was equivalent to healing the Earth – the restoration of right and order. Maintaining right and order, to prevent the world from falling into chaos was central to the pharaoh's (rulers of ancient Egypt) role.

Asia

Persia

One of the earliest routes for early human migrations out of Africa was through Nile Valley to Greater Iran. This Iranian plateau, including central Asian and Caucasian highlands, had a wide range of geographic resources supporting early hominids who wandered into the region. Evidence suggests hunter-gatherer early humans, including Neanderthals living mainly in caves in this region before 200,000 years from now. Modern humans most likely arrived there sometime before 40,000 YA and interbred with the Neanderthals, Homo Heilderbergensis and Denisovans, already living there.

The Persians were migratory people who referred to themselves as Aryan, meaning "noble" or "free", and had nothing to do with race. One branch, Indo-Iranians, settled in and around the region now known as Iran 5000 years back. Another group moved further east and settled in the Indus Valley and are known as Indo-Aryans.

Creation & the Problem of Evil

The world, seen and unseen, was created by Ahura Mazda, the source of all good and life. Ahura Mazda was eternal and, by his goodness, made all that was known in seven steps: Sky, Water, Earth, Plants (vegetation, crops), Animals, Human Beings and Fire.

The sky was an orb suspended amid nothingness. Ahura Mazda released waters within it and then separated the waters from each other by the Earth. The sky element rose high above the Earth and passed beneath it.

Ahura Mazda spread all different kinds of vegetation and imbued it with its own life upon the Earth. He then created Gavaevodta, the Primordial Bull, who gave life to all other animals to feed on and fertilise the vegetation. Once animals and plant life were in place, Ahura Mazda created the first man, Gayomartan, who was beautiful and "bright as the sun". This attracted the attention of Angra Mainyu, the evil who killed him.

The Sun then purified and planted Gayomartan's seed in the ground. Forty years later, a rhubarb plant came out and grew into the first mortal couple – Mashya and Mashyanag. Ahura Mazda breathed the spirit of life into them, which became their souls. Mashya and Mashyanag lived in complete harmony with each other, the world's animals, and Ahura Mazda.

Soon, Angra Mainyu came into their paradise. He seduced them by claiming that he was their creator and master of the world and that Ahura Mazda had been deceiving them. Confused, the couple doubted their actual creator's word and accepted the lie of Angra Mainyu. So, sin entered the world, and harmony was lost.

The couple did not conceive for 50 years after their fall into sin. When Mashyanag finally gave birth, she and Mashya ate their children because they had lost all sense of balance and reason. Many years after this, another set of twins was born who became the ancestors of humanity. But because the first couple accepted Angra Mainyu's lie, paradise was lost, and humans will have now to live in conflict with the natural world and each other.

Humans were granted the gift of free will by Ahura Mazda. They could choose to believe Angra Mainyu's lies over their creator's truth. So, the meaning of human existence comes down to exercising that free will in choosing good over evil. What one chooses would then dictate the quality of one's life and, naturally, one's afterlife.

Sumer

Sumer was an ancient civilisation founded in the Mesopotamia region of the fertile crescent situated between the Tigris and Euphrates rivers (now southern Iraq). Sumerians are considered the creators of modern human civilisation, known for their language, governance, architecture, and innovations. Humans first settled in Mesopotamia more than 16,000 years from now. Later they formed farming communities following the domestication of animals and the development of agriculture with irrigation from the Tigris and Euphrates rivers.

Sumerian creation story

The earliest record of a Sumerian creation myth, called The Eridu Genesis, was found on a single fragmentary tablet excavated in Nippur. It is written in the Sumerian language and dated to over 3500 years back. The beginning of the tablet is lost. No Sumerian story describes creation; the existence of the gods is simply assumed. There was no concept of a beginning void. The powers of the cosmos were thought to have always existed.

The goddess Namma, a deity of the underground waters, gave birth to the Universe. Heaven and Earth (conceived as both male and female) are created by Enlil, the head of all gods. In its beginnings, the Earth was dark; no light or vegetation existed, and no water emerged from the deep.

Birth of Mankind: Heaven and Earth were already separated. At that time, after the gods had produced more offspring, there was a shortage of food. The minor gods were assigned to farming to grow food. To do so, they had the tiring job of digging and dredging the canals first. The work was so hard and challenging that the junior gods complained. When that did not work, they decided to rebel.

The senior God Enki was fast asleep at the time and was roused from his slumber. He realised the need for a creative solution. Enki decides to create humankind. The goddess Namma was asked to knead clay from the fresh waters under the Earth, mix it with the blood of one of the gods killed, and place it in her womb. She then gave birth to the first humans. Humans from then on have taken up the burden of working the soil and creating produce.

Enlil, the air-God, then brought forth trees and grain to establish abundance and prosperity in the land. For this, the brothers Emesh and Enten were created. Enten made the ewe give birth to the lamb and the goat to give birth to the kid. He made cows multiply with calves. Much of fat and milk was produced. In the plain, the wild goat, the sheep, and the donkey were made. Enten also made the birds of heaven set up nests in the wide Earth. He had the fish of the sea lay their eggs in the swampland. He made the palm-grove and vineyard abundant with honey and wine. The trees, wherever planted, Enten made them bear fruit. Grain and crops he made to multiply.

Emesh brought into existence the trees and the fields. He made vast stables and sheepfolds. In the farms, he multiplied the produce. The (missing words in the tablet) . . . he caused to cover the Earth, -----
The abundant harvest he made was brought into the houses, which made the granaries heaped high.

Enki went to the Tigris and Euphrates Rivers. He filled them with sparkling water and appointed the God Enbilulu in charge of rivers. Enki then filled the rivers with fish and made the "son of Kesh" responsible for them. He next turned to the sea (Persian Gulf), set up its rules, and appointed the goddess Sirara in charge.

India

The peopling of the Indian Subcontinent with Homo Sapiens took place in multiple waves of migrations from Africa over tens of millennia.

By some 70-50,000 years ago, a small group crossed the Red Sea, possibly less than 1,000 people. They travelled along the coast of Arabia and Persia until reaching India, Sri Lanka and the Andaman Islands. They continued their journey then to southeast Asia. It was the first major settling point of modern humans out of Africa.

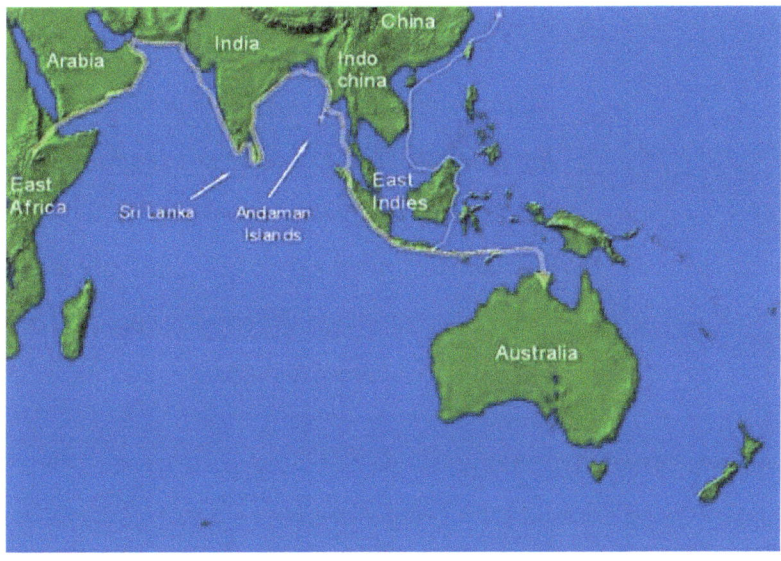

The southern route of human migration out of Africa

Later the Indo-Aryans may have arrived in India between 7500 – 6200 years back, migrating into north-western India from Persia and then to inner Asia.

Mysteries of Creation

An unknown poet in India before the Vedic age (1500 – 500 BC) wrote:

There was neither existence nor non-existence,

The kingdom of the air, nor the sky beyond.

What was there to contain, to cover in—

Was it but vast, unfathomed depths of water?

There was no death there, nor immortality.

No sun was there, dividing day from night.

Then was there only that,

Resting within itself.

Apart from it, there was not anything.

At first, within the darkness veiled in darkness,

Chaos unknowable, the All lay hidden.

Till, straightway from the formless void made manifest

By the great power of heat was born that germ.

From Rigveda

The poet then says that wise men had discovered in their hearts that the germ of Being existed in Not Being. But who, he asked, could tell how Being first originated? The gods came later and are unable to reveal how creation began. He who guards the Universe knows, or maybe he does not know.

Santals

The Santals (from "sons of mankind") are the speaker of one of the oldest languages of India. They are the third-largest tribe in India and are found in the states of West Bengal, Bihar, Orissa, Jharkhand and Assam. Anthropologists think they entered India well before the Aryans invasions, by way of Assam and Bengal, as their traditions indicate.

Santal creation story

In the beginning, there was only water, and underneath it was soil. First, Thakur Jiu (Supreme God) created fishes, tortoises, crocodiles, earthworms, Sun, Moon, and all kinds of living creatures of the water. Then, he started to create humans. Thakur Jiu asked for help from the female creator, Malin Budhi. She made two human bodies from clay and foam in a rock cave underwater and laid them out to dry. The day-horse, Singh Sadom, was passing that way and trampled the model.

Thakur Jiu asked the pieces to be kicked into the water. With Thakur Jiu, Malin

Budhi tried again. But at this second attempt, there was another hitch. He had left the human spirits on top of a door frame next to the spirits for the birds. Malin Budhi being short, fetched the wrong ones.   When animated, their models turned into two birds, Has and Hasil (meaning goose and gander), who flew away over the seas for twelve years looking for somewhere to nest.

Thakur Jiu asked many sea creatures to raise the land above the sea, but all were unsuccessful. Finally, the earthworm, which had swallowed Earth only to pass it out from its other end, suggested asking Prince Tortoise from the sea. The land under the sea was hitched up by chains to the turtle, and he raised an island.

Thakur Jiu planted grass and trees on the island. This was the creation of dharti (the Earth), pataal (the abyss), cows, bulls, saal trees, mahua, and various other plants. The birds, Has and Hasil, landed and laid their eggs, which were then eaten twice by 'Raghop Buar'. Thakur Jiu then sent 'Jaer-era' to guard the eggs. Finally, the eggs hatched to produce two human beings, a male and female 'Pilchu Haram' and 'Pilchu Budhi', who were the earliest humans.

The first human couple grew up in "Hihiri Pipiri, the original birthplace of the Santals, which was a place like a paradise. The first human beings were taken care of by the birds according to the advice of Thakur jiu. Soon the birds were facing difficulties to find enough and the right kind of feed for the first human couple.

They prayed to Thakur Jiu, who created the whole Universe for the wellbeing of humankind. There were enough fruits and other food for all. Soon Thakur Jiu brought into existence a cow that gave milk to them. The cow gave birth to two bulls, and the humans were taught how to plough the land with them. They planted millet and rice. When they were ripe and collected, the humans cleared their house with cow dung. Then facing east, they gave their first offering to Thakur Jiu with their harvest.

The first man and woman lived in joy and happiness under the loving care and protection of God. They talked with Him and had fellowship with Him.

Santals took it for granted that God was with humankind from the beginning of creation. Santals believe that the Supreme God has a living and intimate relationship with all human beings, here in this world and in the life after death. They believe that the present life does not end with death, and the life after death is in God's hand. He will take them to the next world.

Muria people

Muria tribe belongs to the Gond people (largest tribal group in India) of Central India. They dance to the music of buffalo-horn trumpet, the hakum, and varying types of drums called mandri, kotoloka and kundir during their joyful harvest festivals.

Earth and the sky

A long, long time ago, the sky and the Earth, husband, and wife, lived together. There was no sun or the Moon as the clouds were right above the ground. Clouds were more and more coming closer to the Earth, curious about all things on Earth.

Humans were gradually becoming tiny, squeezed between the Earth and the cloud. They were so small that they had to use rats to plough their fields instead of bulls. If they wanted to pluck any vegetables like tomatoes or aubergines, they had to stand on tiptoe to reach them on the trees, just like plucking mangoes now. Life was tough as their heads kept banging against the clouds when they tried to walk upright. They were frustrated and fed up.

One day, a very old granny was sweeping her courtyard. As she moved to clean with the broom, her elbow hit against the cloud. Hurt with the impact, *this time, the granny lost her temper. She clouted the cloud hard with her broom. Scared of her, the cloud with the sky flung like a rocket and reached up, where it is today. And from then on, the Sun and Moon could also be seen between the clouds and the sky.*

Humans were finally relieved and started growing tall ever since.

Hindu

The word Hindu is derived from the Indo-Aryan and Sanskrit word Sindhu, which means a large body of water. The term Hindu came from a Persian term for the people who lived beyond the river Indus. Hinduism contains a broad range of philosophies. The Puranas are Hindu religious texts in India composed in Sanskrit, orally narrated for centuries before being written down from around 2000 years ago.

Story of Prajapati and Churning of the Sea

After Mahāpralaya, the great dissolution of the Universe, there was darkness everywhere. Everything was in a state of sleep. There was nothing, either moving or static.

Then Svayambhu, self-manifested Being, arose, which is a form beyond senses. Svayambhu first created the vast and endless depth of primordial waters and established its seed. The seed turned into a golden womb, Hiraṇyagarbha. Over

time these endless waters produced a single golden egg.
Then Svayambhu entered the egg.

The egg floated on the surface for nine months. After nine months, the eggshell cracked open, and Prajapati was standing in its middle. Prajapati was neither male nor female but the all-powerful combination of both. Prajapati rested on the golden shell for almost a year without speaking or moving.

After one year, Prajapati broke the silence – the first word he said became the Earth. The next word spoken became the sky, which he divided into seasons.

Prajapati became lonely and wanted a mate in his loneliness and divided into two beings, a male and a female. Together they created the gods, the elements and mankind. When Prajapati inhaled, he made the devas (gods), fire and light. When he exhaled, he created the asuras (demons) and darkness.

Then, together with the goddess of language, he made all beings and time. The first to be born then was Agni – the God of fire. Once there was fire, there was light. Prajapati separated light into day and night. Other gods were born, including the beautiful Dawn (Usha). Next, Prajapati separated evil from good and hid the evil offsprings deep into the Earth.

The gods had weakened a long time ago when their most precious treasures were lost beneath the primordial ocean due to the great deluge. Significant amongst these was the loss of Amrita, the nectar of immortality and Lakshmi, the goddess of fortune and wealth. These treasures - the elixir of immortality and Lakshmi - were vital for the gods to successfully conquer the demons who had taken over the Universe by then.

They needed to act quickly. So Vishnu, the preserver god of the Hindu Trimurti (the Trinity), advised the gods to churn the ocean and recover all the treasures. Vishnu knew the gods would be unable to do this by themselves. He struck a deal with the demons. He promised them a share of the treasures, including Amrita, if they would help churn. The demons agreed.

Vishnu told the gods and demons they should use Mount Mandhara as a churning stick and Vasuki, the giant king of the serpent, as a rope. He also persuaded the demons to hold the snake's head, spitting furiously, while the gods had the tail end. The serpent was then coiled around the mountain. Each side alternately pulled the rope and then relaxed, causing the mountain to rotate in the water. To regain the treasures, they worked very hard. But there were many problems they had to face.

The demons (asuras) were poisoned by fumes coming out of Vasuki's breath that grew very hot, and the demons almost suffocated. Still, they all continued their work by pulling back and forth on the snake's body all the time. The churning continued, but Mt Mandhara began to sink into the soft sand bed of the sea. At once, Lord Vishnu assumed the form of a turtle and held the mountain from sinking. Then, he placed the mountain on his back to act as a foundation stone, thus allowing the churning to continue.

Finally, several wonderful treasures sprung out of the ocean. But before that, the deadly poison, halahala, from Vasuki's mouth came out. It began to threaten the very existence of all. It was crucial to remove it as it could contaminate the Milky Ocean and destroy all creation. On the advice of Lord Vishnu, the gods approached Lord Shiva for help and rotection. Shiva inhaled the poison in the act of self-sacrifice. The colour of Lord Shiva's neck turned blue. That is why he is often called 'Nilakanta' (the blue-throated one). But he successfully stopped the poison from spreading

When Amrita, the elixir of immortality, finally came to the surface, the demons rushed to grab it. Now, it was Vishnu's turn to help. He assumed the form of Mohini, a beautiful woman who captivated all the demons.   She changed the elixir for alcohol by sleight of hand and returned the precious liquid to the gods. Thus, the Amrita was secured only for the gods.

However, one of the cunning demons, Rahu, disguised as a god, at last, managed to get a taste of Amrita. The Sun and the Moon warned Vishnu, who immediately cut off Rahu's head. But the demon had already consumed some of the Amrita to make him immortal. Ever since his head is known as Rahu, and his corpse is Ketu. They became the most potent enemy of the Sun and Moon. Because of this, Sun and Moon eclipses occur as Rahu and Ketu swallow Sun and Moon when they come close to each other.

Soon the ocean revealed all other precious treasures. Among them was Lakshmi, a beautiful woman standing on a lotus flower. Seeing all the gods before her, she chose the God she felt was most worthy of her, the great Vishnu. Lakshmi and Vishnu became inseparable - forever.

The Big Bang Theory is the current scientific effort to explain how our Universe came into existence. The Vedic rishis, seer scientists of their times in India, 4000 years ago, also asked the same question. In the *Rig Veda,* it is asked, "How was this Universe created? Who created it?" Indeed, the science written in the Vedas was as profound as it was poetic. The Vedas, meaning "knowledge," are the oldest texts of the Hinduism culture of the Indian Subcontinent. It began as an oral tradition passed down through generations before finally being written in Vedic Sanskrit between 3600- 2600 YA.

"There was neither Aught nor Naught...
No air nor sky
What covered all? Where rested all?

A void in wrapth...
Who knows ... from whence this vast creation arose?

No Gods had then been born
Who then can ever the truth disclose?

Whence sprang the world
Whether framed by hand divine or no,
Lord in heaven alone can tell
If even He can show.

This then goes on to explain the concept of Creation:

"That alone, by its own power breathed without air.
Besides or beyond That one, there was nothing.
Darkness was further shrouded by darkness
which appeared to flow all around.
That One came to be, even from this emptiness,
by the power of its own intent.
Within That One appeared the first seed of mind
in which arose
an impulse of diffusion and concentration power.
These rays of concentrated power spread
on all sides in the manifested mass
slanting below as well as up
and in the sides everywhere.
From these rays of power arose the seeds of mind,
and they became greater.
The power of the seeds of mind remained concentrated in them
while the pressure of concussion remained on the other side.

The science in the Vedas goes deeper.

Nobody can describe the process of creation
Gods cannot describe the process of creation
because they also did not see the process of creation,
They came into existence only after the visible world had happened.

China

The first humans to leave Africa travelled to Asia, not Europe. A discovery in southern China of human teeth dated to around 100,000 years back indicates Homo sapiens was possibly present in the region considerably earlier than previously suspected. This was possibly from the earlier waves of human migration. It is now thought Homo sapiens arrived in China at least 55,000 YA.

Pan Gu and the Egg of the World

First written down about 1,760 years ago, this story of how the Universe began was told orally long before that.

Long, long ago—not in a land before time, but a time before land—there was nothing in the Universe except an enormous egg-shaped entity. Inside the "egg," the opposing forces of yin and yang were all scrambled in a complete mess. But over time, the interactions between various substances and energies eventually conceived a being—a shaggy, horned giant named Pan Gu. For 18,000 years, Pan Gu slept and grew. One day, he suddenly awoke. When he opened his eyes, he saw only darkness.

He strained his ears but heard only unnerving silence. Pan Gu found these dreary surroundings highly disturbing. Conjuring a magical axe, he landed a mighty chop upon the egg. The egg split into two with a thunderous crack. Slowly, yin and yang began to separate. Everything dark and heavy sank down to form the Earth. And the rest, light and clear, drifted up to create the heavens. He split chaos into opposites in the Earth and in the sky.

Pan Gu stood in the middle, his head touching the sky, his feet planted on Earth. Anxious that the halves would close up again, he stood between the two halves to keep them apart. With each passing day, the sky rose 10 feet further above him, the Earth thickened 10 feet below, and Pan Gu himself grew along with them, just to keep up with the growing expanse and hold on.

After another 18,000 years, the sky was higher, and Earth was thicker. Pan Gu stood between them like a pillar 30,000 miles in height, so they would never again join. It was a lonely and strenuous job.

The unselfish giant endured this toil for another six million five hundred and seventy thousand days (18,000 years) until he was sure that the realms were finally stabilised. Then with a great crash, Pan Gu lay down and died. As Pan Gu died, a miraculous transformation took place. His final breath turned into winds and clouds, his voice into rumbling thunder. Pan Gu's skull became the top of the sky; his hair and beard became stars of the Milky Way. His one eye became the Sun and the other the Moon.

Pan Gu's limbs transformed into great mountains, and the blood running through his veins into flowing rivers. His flesh converted into fertile farmlands, and his bones turned to precious gems and minerals. Pan Gu's teeth and nails became lustrous metals; the hairs on his skin burgeoned into lush vegetation. And the sweat from his extended labours fell as rainwater for the mortal world.

Some people say that the fleas and the lice on his body became the ancestors of humans. Others say that Pan Gu's spirit never ceased but turned into humans, which accounts for the ancient Chinese belief that humans are the soul of all matter.

Mongolia

Modern humans travelled across the Eurasian steppe north of the Asian high mountains to reach Mongolia and northern China about 45,000 years ago.

Esege Malan and Mother Earth

There knows are, as everyone, people in the sky as well as on the Earth. They existed long before we did—no one knows how long. The oldest and chief of those people was Esege Malan, who lived in the sky.

Ehé Tazar, Mother Earth, went to visit him and spent several delightful days together. When Ehé Tazar was ready to return to the Earth, she asked Esege Malan to give her the Sun and the Moon. Esege Malan was happy to give them to her, but he soon found it very difficult to get them for her. He called a thousand Burkans together and asked how this could be done. Although they thought for long and earnestly, they did not have an answer.

Then Esege Malan sent for Esh (the hedgehog) to come up to his place in the sky. Esh was very wise but was footless. He had initially refused to come to the meeting because he was afraid of being laughed at because he had no feet.

Esege Malan had three daughters who often came down to the Earth. There they removed their clothing, turned themselves into swans, and swam in the water. As it happened, the three were at home with Esege Malan when Esh had come up after repeated requests. Esege had told his daughters that Esh was odd. He was lame and hairy but very wise, and they must not laugh at him. But when Esh walked in, Esege's daughters looked sidewise and laughed. They could not help it; he was so comical.

Esh saw them laugh and said to himself, "Esege Malan has called me up here for his daughters to laugh at and ridicule me!" He became terribly angry and left so quickly that Esege had no time to say a word. Esh knew, however, what

Esege wanted, for the messenger had told him. When Esh came down from the sky, two Shalmos (invisible spirits) followed, sent by Esege Malan to listen and hear what Esh said as he travelled. For Esege knew that Esh was raging, and he thought he might still say something about the Sun and the Moon.

The first thing Esh saw as he came to Earth was a herd of cows and bulls. When they caught sight of him, they were frightened, put up their tails and ran. Esh, angry that they should be frightened at him, cursed them, saying: "May the hair rope never leave your nostrils, and the yoke never leaves your necks!" And so, it has been since.

He went farther and came to a herd of horses. They were frightened too and raised their tails and ran away. Esh, terribly angry, cursed them, "May the metal bit never leave your mouths, and the saddle never leaves your backs!" And so, it has been.

The Shalmos followed him constantly, listening to what he said.

After a time, Esh began to talk to himself and abuse Esege Malan. "What sort of a ruler is that Esege Malan?" asked he. "What sort of a master of the world? He manages everything, fixes everything. He has agreed to give away the Sun and the Moon but does not know how to get them! If he is so wise, why does he not come to visit Mother Earth? When the visit is ended, he can ask her for the hot dancing air of summer and the echo, habra yirligin and darbon. She would want to give them to him gladly, but how could she get them for him? That way, they will be equal. "

When the Shalmos heard this, they followed no farther but quickly went to the sky and told Esege Malan everything Esh had said.

Esege waited until a sufficient time had passed; then he came to return Mother Earth's visit. While they were walking, he said: "When you came to visit me, I gave you the Sun and the Moon, now I ask for a present. Give me the hot dancing air of summer and echo." She was happy to give them to him, but try as she would, she could not get them for him.

When she found that it was impossible to get them, and no one could tell her how to do it, Esege said: "Let the Sun and the Moon remain where they are, and the hot dancing air of summer and echo stay here!"

And so it is that though the Sun and the Moon belong to the Earth, they are in the sky, and the hot dancing air and the echo, though they belong to Esege Malan, remain with Mother Earth.

Japan

Modern humans first arrived in Japan around 35,000 to 40,000 years ago. They came possibly following great herds of animals across land bridges connecting Japanese islands with the Asian continent and also on boats via the chain of islands linking southern Japanese islands.

Japanese creation story

Long ago, all the elements were mixed together with one germ of life. This germ began to mix things around and around until the heavier part sank and the lighter part rose. A muddy sea that covered the entire Earth was created. From this ocean grew a green shoot. It grew and grew until it reached the clouds and was transformed into a god. Soon this God grew lonely, and it began to create other gods. The last two gods it made, Izanagi and Izanami, were the most remarkable.

One day as they were walking along, they looked down on the ocean and wondered what was beneath it. Izanagi thrust his staff into the waters, and as he pulled it back up, some clumps of mud fell back into the sea. They began to harden and grow until they became the islands of Japan.

The two descended to these islands and began to explore, each going in different directions. They created all kinds of plants. When they met again, they decided to marry and have children to inhabit the land Izanami created the gods of the sea, river, mountain, field, tree, stone, fire and many others. But in giving birth to the fire god, she was burned and died. Izanagi waited long for Izanami's return. Then he entered the palace of the gods of Yomi, the land of the dead, only to find Izanami's corpse horribly disfigured. He fled, pursued by the shamed Izanami, and escaped by blocking the exit of Yomi with a large boulder.

Izanagi then went to the river to purify himself by bathing. When Izanagi washed his left eye, Amaterasu Omikami (Goddess of the Sun) was born. When Izanagi washed his right eye, Tsukuyomi no Mikoto (God of the Moon) was born. When he cleaned his nose, Susanoo no Mikoto (God of storms) came from *his nose. Izanagi charged Amaterasu Omikami with the rule of the High Plain of Heaven, Tsukushi no Mikoto with the Realm of Night, and Susanoo no Mikoto with the Plain of the Seas.*

Thus, was born Japan and its surrounding world.

South-East Asia

Homo Sapiens migrated from East Africa approximately 70,000 – 50,000 YA and spread along the southern coast of Asia, reaching South East Asia and Oceania about 60,000 - 50,000 YA.

Creation Story from Lake Toba, Sumatra, Indonesia

Sideak Parujar was a goddess who escaped from her lizard-like would-be husband. She came down on a spun thread from the sky, the world of gods, to a middle world which then was only shapeless waters. It was not comfortable there, but she resolved not to go back to the sky.

Her caring grandfather sent her a handful of Earth that she spread to make it broad and long. Unknowingly, she put the Earth on the head of a monstrous dragon, Naga Padoha, who lived in the waters of the underworld.

The monster was not pleased and attempted to get rid of the Earth, covering his head by rolling around, making Sideak Parujar's life quite miserable. Resourceful Sideak Parujar plunged a sword into the dragon's body up to the hilt and immobilised the monster.

Even this day, when Naga Padoha twists in his restraint, an earthquake rumbles throughout the land.

Lake Toba is a large natural lake in North Sumatra, Indonesia, occupying the caldera of a supervolcano that erupted 75,000 years back, changing the course of human migration history.

Kidul myth from the folklore of Yogyakarta, Java

Long ago, there was a beautiful woman named Kadita. She was the daughter of Prabu Munding Wangi. Kadita was the favourite of the entire kingdom, especially the local people. She was so beautiful that she was called Dewi Srengenge, or beautiful Sun. Her royal father doted on his daughter.

Even though Prabu Munding Wangi had a beautiful daughter, he longed for a son to inherit his throne. Without a son, to him and according to the law of the land, there was not a proper successor to the throne. Eventually, he married Poetri Moentiara and had a son with his second wife. Poetri Moentiara was very jealous of Kadita and her mother. She begged the king to banish both her rivals from the court. However, Prabu Munding Wangi loved his first wife and daughter and didn't do as she had asked.

The new queen Poetri Moentiara had her sights set on the throne for her son.

She viewed Kadita as a threat and attempted to remove her from the kingdom. She tried to oust Kadita, but this only enraged Munding. Poetri Moentiara then called upon the renowned witch, Djahil. She promised her a princely reward if Dewi Kadita and her mother were banished. Djahil thought for a moment and incanted a rapal (spell). Soon both mother and daughter began to suffer a dreadful skin disease with a foul smell.

This made Kadita sad and cry hysterically. The king asked for the best healers of the kingdom to treat his daughter. Sadly, her illness could not be treated with traditional medicine. He eventually realised her disease was from a mystical source.

According to the law, the mother and the daughter were banished to the wild forest high on the mountain. With a heavy heart, King Munding Wangi saw the two set off on their way to the forest, covered in terrible sores. A great sadness fell across the land, except for Poetri Moentiara, the king's second wife, who had achieved her aim.

The princess kadita and her mother fell on hard times. In the forest lived a hermit who took pity on them and fortunately provided food and shelter in a cave temple. But Kadita's mother died shortly, and she was all alone in the world. As much as he tried, the hermit could not help with Kadita's weeping sores and emotional pain.

Kadita soon left the mountain and travelled southward from village to village, further and further, until eventually, she reached the shores of the Southern Sea. She climbed up on a high cliff and gazed out onto the sea that spread before her. Gazing at the cold blue water, she was able to momentarily *forget all her pain and suffering.*

Suddenly awaking from these thoughts, she jumped into the deep and swam towards the middle. After reaching the centre of the sea, she noticed her sores had vanished from her skin, the foul smell was gone, and she had become more beautiful. The gods watching her hardships were filled with deep compassion. So, they transformed Kadita into a powerful spirit of the netherworld, Ratu Kidul. To this day, she resides in her grand palace under the sea.

Dayak creation story, Malay

It tells that the attempt to create humans also gave birth to orang-utans, which means "people of the forest" in Malay. We know now that Orang-Utans share 97% of human genes and are possibly the closest living relatives to modern humans.

After the two birds, Iri and Ringgon, had formed the earth, plants, and animals, they decided to create humans.

At first, they made humans from clay, but he could neither speak nor move when he was dried. This made them upset, and they ran at him angrily. He was so frightened that he fell backwards and broke all to pieces.

The next man Iri and Ringgon made was of hardwood. But he was utterly stupid and absolutely good for nothing. Then the two birds searched carefully for the perfect material and eventually selected the wood of the Kampong tree. Its wood has a strong fibre and exudes a quantity of deep red sap whenever it is cut.

Out of this tree, they fashioned a man and a woman. They were so well pleased with this achievement that to celebrate, they feasted late into the night. The next day they tried to make more humans, but not feeling so well after the night's party, they messed up the recipe and ended up creating Orang-Utans instead.

Australia

Outside Africa, Australia has one of the longest histories of continuous human occupation, dating back about 50,000 years. Around 50,000 years ago, humans reached "Sahul" from South East Asia by boat, thousands of years before the arrival of European colonists. This prehistoric supercontinent initially united New Guinea, Australia, and Tasmania, until these regions were separated by rising sea levels approximately 10,000 years ago. Original occupants of the land were later called (Ab)Original, from the Latin phrase *ab origine,* which meant 'from the beginning'.

Background of the Aboriginal people –

the Occupants of the Land

Living mainly along the shores, they fished and hunted in the waters and harvested food from the surrounding bush. Moving throughout their country following the seasons, they only needed to spend a few hours per day working to ensure their survival. With such a large amount of leisure time available, they developed a rich and complex ritual life – language, customs, spirituality and the law – the heart of which was the connection to the land.

Over 20,000 years old Aboriginal cave paintings in Ubirr

Aboriginal Creation story

There was a time when everything was still. All the spirits of the earth were asleep, except the great Father of All Spirits. Gently he woke up the Sun Mother. When she opened her eyes, a warm ray of light spread out towards the sleeping earth. The Father of All Spirits said to the Sun Mother, "Go down to the Earth and awake the sleeping spirits. Give them forms."

The Sun Mother glided down to Earth, which was bare at the time and began to walk in all directions. Everywhere she walked, plants grew. After returning to the field where she had started her work, the Mother rested, well pleased with herself.

The Father of All Spirits later instructed her to go into the caves and wake the spirits. The Mother went into the dark caves on the mountainsides. The bright light that radiated from her awoke the spirits. As she left, insects of all kinds flew out of the caves. The Sun Mother sat down and watched the glorious sight of her insects, mingling with her flowers.

But once again, the Great Father urged her on. The Mother ventured into a very deep icy cave, spreading her light around her. Her heat melted the ice. The rivers and streams of the world were now created. Then she made fish and small snakes, lizards, and frogs. Next, she awoke the spirits of the birds and animals, and they burst into the sunshine in a dazzling array of colours. The Father of All Spirits was pleased with the Sun Mother's work.

She called all her creatures to her and instructed them to enjoy the earth's wealth and live peacefully with one another. Then she rose into the sky and became the sun. The living creatures watched the sun in awe as she crept across the sky, towards the west. But when she finally sunk beneath the western horizon, they became panic-stricken, thinking she had deserted them. All night they stood frozen in their places, imagining that the end of time had come. But after a very long time, the Sun Mother raised her head above the horizon in the East. The earth's children learned to expect her coming and going and were no longer afraid.

At first, the creatures lived together peacefully, but eventually, envy crept into their hearts. They began to argue. The Sun Mother was forced to come down from the sky to mediate their bickering. She gave each creature the power to change their form to whatever they chose. But she was not pleased with the end result. The rats she had made had transformed into bats; there were giant lizards and fish with blue tongues and feet. However, the oddest of the new animals were an animal with a duck-like bill, teeth for chewing, tail like a beaver, and it laid eggs. It was called the platypus.

The Sun Mother looked down upon the Earth and thought that she must create new creatures; otherwise, the Father of All Spirits will not be happy with what he will see. She gave birth to two children, the Morning Star and the Moon goddess. They had two children, and these she sent to Earth. They became our ancestors. She made them superior to the animals because they had part of her mind and would never want to change their shape.

Papua New Guinea

With only around 9 million people, Papua New Guinea has more languages than any other country in the world, over 800 indigenous languages, 12% of the total languages in the world. Most of these languages have only around 1000 speakers. In Papua New Guinea, in traditional societies, mountains animate a sense of awe and malevolence. And they are also recognised as a source of life, spirituality and identity.

All cultures and religions have their creation stories. Kaluli tribes live in the middle of the virgin rainforest on the collapsed cone of an extinct volcano, Mt Bosavi, one of the remotest places on earth.

Kaluli Creation story

Kaluli people believe everything in the world was created to solve the problems of cold and hunger. They think that all things had their origin at a time in the distant past known as hena madaliaki (meaning "when the land came into form").

During hena madaliaki, there were no trees or animals or streams or sago or food. The earth was covered entirely by people. These people soon became hungry and cold as they had nothing to eat or anything to build houses with.

One old man got up and said, "Everyone, gather around here."

When everyone had come together, he said to one group, "You be trees," and that group of people became trees.

"You be sago," he said to another group, and they became sago.

"You be fish…. You be bananas," and so on. Until, all the animals, plants and every other being in the world, like rivers, hills were divided each to his own kind.

The few people who were left became the human beings of today.

This Kaluli myth is known as *"alo bana hanan*—the splitting of the house." The significance of this runs deeper, referring to the fundamental relationship among all things in the world.

New Zealand

New Zealand is a young country in terms of its human history. The first people to arrive in New Zealand were ancestors of the Māori. They probably arrived from Polynesia by boats only between 900 and 800 years back. Although the first European to set foot there later was in 1642, a long time passed — 127 years — before New Zealand was visited by another European.

Maori legends

In Polynesian mythology, people, the elements and every aspect of nature are descended from one original pair, the Sky Father and the Earth Mother. It was for this reason that the ancient Maori identified themselves so closely with nature. Felling a tree was like slaying a child of Tane Mahuta, god of the forest, and they would appease the spirits for this.

In the beginning, there was only darkness, Te Ponui, Te Poroa (the Great Night, the Long Night). At last, a glow appeared in the void of empty space, the moon and the sun sprang forth, and the heavens were made light.

Then Rangi (the Sky Father) lived with Papa (the Earth Mother), but their offspring lived in darkness as the two clung together. The Sky lay upon the Earth, but the light had not yet come between them.

Their children were frustrated that they could not see. They argued among themselves as to how night and day might be made to appear. The fierce Tumatauenga (god of war) urged them to kill their parents. But TaneMahuta (god of the forests) advised that they separate their father Rangi from their mother Papa to achieve their goal.

Tane's wisdom prevailed, and in turn, each of the children struggled mightily to separate the Sky from the Earth. Rongo (god of cultivated food) and Tangaroa (god of the sea) did all they could. The belligerent Tumatauenga cut and hacked. But to no avail. Finally, Tane Mahuta, by thrusting with his mighty feet, gradually lifted the anguished Rangi away from the agonised Papa. The Sky was separated from the Earth.

Heartbroken, Rangi shed tears, so much so that the oceans were formed. Tawhiri (god of wind and storm), who had opposed his brothers in the venture, feared Papa was becoming too beautiful. He followed his father to the sky above. From there, he swept down furiously to lash the trees of Tane Mahuta, which were uprooted and fell in disarray.

Tawhiri then turned his rage on Tangaroa (god of the sea), who sought refuge in the depths of the ocean. But as Tangaroa fled, his many grandchildren were confused, and while the fish swam to the seas with him, the lizards and reptiles hid among rocks and the battered forests.

It was then for Tangaroa to show his anger. His grandchildren had deserted him and were sheltering in the woods. So it is that even to this day, the sea is eating into the land, slowly eroding it. Tangaroa is still hoping that the forests will disappear in time, and he will be reunited with his offspring.

The creation of woman: When all of them lay exhausted and peace at last descended, Tane Mahuta fashioned a woman's body from clay and breathed life into her nostrils. She became Hine-hauone (the Earth-formed Maid) and bore Tane Mahuta a daughter, Hine-titama (the Dawn Maid), who in time also had daughters.

But Hine-titama did not know who her father was. When she found he was the Tane she thought was her husband, she was overwhelmed with shame. She left Te Ao (the world of light) and moved to Te Po (the world below). There she became known as Hinenui-te-Po (Great Hine the Night). Tane had many children, and they increased and multiplied, for death held no dominion over them.

The birth of Maui: The fifth of his parents' sons, Maui, was born so premature, frail, and underdeveloped that he could not possibly have survived. His mother, Taranga, wrapped the foetus in a knot of her hair and threw it into the sea. Hence Maui's full name of Maui-tikitiki-a-Taranga (Maui, the topknot of Taranga). Indeed, he would have died, but the gods intervened and Rangi, the Sky Father, nursed him through infancy. As a grown child, Maui returned to confront his bewildered mother and to amaze his family with feats of magic.

The snaring of the sun: Maui's four brothers were then jealous of the favouritism shown to him. But when Maui offered to slow down the sun so that the days would be longer and they would all have more time to find food, they agreed to work with him. Carrying the enchanted jawbone of his grandmother, Maui led his brothers eastwards to the edge of the pit from which the sun rises each morning.

There, as it came up, the brothers snared the sun with huge plaited flax ropes. As they held it still, Maui, with the enchanted jawbone, cruelly smashed the sun's face time and time again. The sun was then so feeble that it could only creep across the sky - and continues so to do to this very day.

Europe

Fossil studies show that between 125,000 YA and 75,000 YA, Homo Sapiens *had* travelled out of Africa a few times and reached Europe, but these earlier migrations appear not to have survived. The first modern humans most likely spread across Europe between 45,000 and 40,000 years back after arriving in Egypt via the northern route out of Africa.

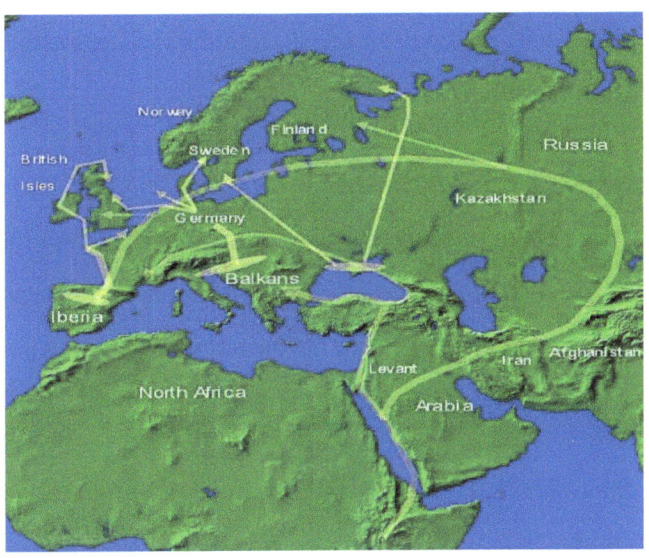

Human migration route out of Africa

Greece

Mycenaean Greece was the last phase of the Bronze Age in Ancient Greece, spanning approximately 3850 to 3150 years ago. The Mycenaean period became the historical setting of much ancient Greek literature and mythology.

Greek creation story

In the beginning, there was only empty darkness. The only thing in this void was Nyx, a bird with black wings. She laid a golden egg with the wind and then sat upon this egg for a long time. Finally, life stirred in the egg and out of it came Eros, the god of love.

One half of the shell went up into the air and became the sky. The other half became the Earth. Eros named the sky Uranus and the Earth he named Gaia. Then Eros made them fall in love.

Uranus and Gaia had many children together and then had grandchildren. Some of their children become scared of the power of the other children. Kronus, to protect himself, reverted to swallowing his children when they were still infants. But his wife Rhea hid their youngest child. She gave Kronus a rock wrapped in swaddling clothes, which he swallowed, thinking it was his son.

Once the child, Zeus, had reached manhood, his mother taught him how to trick his father to give up his brothers and sisters. Once this was done, all the children of Kronus waged a mighty war against their father. After much fighting, the younger generation won. With Zeus as their leader, they began to endow Gaia with life and Uranus with stars.

But soon, the Earth lacked two things: man and animals. Zeus summoned his two sons Prometheus and Epimetheus. He told them to go to Earth and create men and animals and give them each a gift.

Prometheus set to work making men in the image of the gods, while Epimetheus worked on the animals. As Epimetheus worked, he gave each animal he created one of the gifts. After Epimetheus had finished his work, all the gifts were already given away. Prometheus, by then, finally finished making men. But when he went to find what gift to give to mankind, Epimetheus shamefacedly informed him that he had foolishly used up all the gifts on the animals.

Distressed, Prometheus decided he had to give man fire, even though gods were the only ones until then meant to have access to it. As the sun god rode out into the world the following day, Prometheus took some of the fire and brought it to man. He taught his creation how to take care of it and then left them.

When Zeus discovered what Prometheus had done, he became furious. He ordered his son to be chained to a mountain. Then Zeus called a vulture to peck out his liver every day till eternity.

Next, he began to devise a punishment for mankind. Another of his sons created a beautiful woman, Pandora. Each of the gods gave her a gift. Zeus'

present was curiosity and a box which he ordered her never to open. Then he presented Pandora to Epimetheus as a wife.

Pandora's life with Epimetheus was happy except for her intense curiosity to open the box. She was convinced that this gift would also be wonderful because the gods and goddesses had showered her with so many glorious ones. One day when Epimetheus was away, she opened the box.

Out of the box flew all of the horrors which plague the world today - pain, sickness, envy and greed. Pandora screamed loudly. Epimetheus rushed home, hearing Pandora's cry and closed the lid shut. But all of the evils had already escaped into the world.

Later that night, they heard a voice coming from the box saying, "Let me out. I am hope. "Pandora and Epimetheus released her, and she flew out into the world to give hope to humankind.

Slavic region

The present-day Slavic region consists of Russia, Belarus, Ukraine, Poland, Slovakia, Czechoslovakia, Bulgaria, Macedonia, Montenegro, Croatia, Bosnia, Serbia, and Slovenia.

Slavic creation story

At the beginning of the world, God wanted to expand the earth. He called the Devil and told him to dive into the abyss of water to get a handful of soil from there and bring it to him.

Devil thought, he will also make the same land for himself! He dived, took out a handful of earth and stuffed his mouth with it. He brought the soil to God and gave it to him from his hand, but he did not say a word.

God threw the earth, and wherever he threw it, it was suddenly so flat that even when you stand at one end – you can see everything happening at the other end. The devil looked in wonder and wanted to say something but choked. God asked him what did he want? The devil coughed up and ran away in fear.

Then the thunder and lightning struck the running Devil.

From then on, where he will lie down – there will be hills and slides. Where he will cough – there will grow a mountain, where he will jump – there will stick out the celestial mountain. And so, running all over the earth, the devil dug it up: he made hills, slides, mountains, and high mountains.

Creation - a Carpathian carol

It used to be at the beginning of the world –

Then there was no sky or earth,

No sky nor earth but the blue sea,

And in the middle of the sea on oak

Two pigeons were sitting.

Two pigeons on an oak tree

They held such a council,

Happy debated and cooed:

How can we create the world?

We will fall to the bottom of the sea,

We'll bring out the fine sand

Fine sand, bluestone.

We will sow fine sand,

We will pick up the blue pebble.

From fine sand - black earth,

- icy water, green grass.

From the bluestone - the blue sky,

Blue sky, bright sun,

Bright sun, bright moon,

bright moon and all the stars.

Romania

The 42,000 years old skeletal remains of Homo Sapiens found in Romania is considered the earliest known in Europe.

Romanian creation Story

At the beginning of time, all that existed was an infinite ocean called Apa Sâmbetei.

At first, the water was very still and looked like a mirror. Then one day, a ripple appeared, as if someone were gently blowing on it. This created a chain reaction.

As the ripple turned into waves, the foam was created. From the foam, a tree began to grow. The tree was huge, it sprouted branches, and from its branch, a single butterfly and a worm emerged. The butterfly then transformed into a boy, lighting up the world around him. The worm saw this, wriggled and shed his skin, and also became a boy.

The second boy looked at the first and said, "brother!" The first looked at him and said, "I have no brother and no equal. I shall call you non-brother."

The two were known as brother and non-brother, Fîrtat and Nefîrtat, and they created the world.

Fîrtat could not swim, so he asked Nefîrtat to dive to the bottom of the ocean to collect sand to create land. Nefîrtat dove to the bottom, but the sand simply slipped from his fingers. He tried again but failed once more. He dived for the third time, but once again without any luck. Frustrated, Fîrtat said that that was enough, that they would just use the mud from under Nefîrtat's fingernails to create land. Fîrtat used the soil to create an island around the lone tree of their world.

With the island created, Fîrtat thought that it was time to rest. He laid himself down under the tree and began to sleep. Nefîrtat saw his brother resting and believed that this would be the ideal time to take charge. He could get rid of his brother and create the rest of the world himself. Knowing that Fîrtat could not swim, Nefîrtat tried to roll him into the ocean. However, as he rolled his brother, more land appeared. Nefîrtat then tried to move him in the other direction, but more land appeared! Nefîrtat rolled and rolled until every corner of the earth was covered in the ground.

Fîrtat woke up and saw what Nefîrtat had done. He was happy his non-brother had created the rest of the land but thought it was too much. Fîrtat needed to do something to make the world smaller again. The two then grasped the world in their hands, compressing it together. They pressed and pressed, creating creases and ridges, mountains and rivers until the earth was just the right size.

Once the land was created, the two thought it would be best to build a barrier between the waters of the earth and the waters of the heavens. They wanted something that would separate this life from the next and decided to build a sky.

They added the stars, sun, and moon, decorating the sky like a canvas. Suddenly, the sky was too heavy for the earth. There was too much in the sky and nothing to hold it up. Quickly, Nefîrtat dove back into the ocean and made four pillars, supported by four cosmic fish, to hold up the sky.

With sunlight shining down upon the earth, the original tree could now bloom and grow fruit. Fîrtat and Nefîrtat used the fruits to create life. They would pick one fruit and mould it into a different being. This is how men and women, animals, and all other forms of life were created. Fîrtat built beautiful and practical animals, while Nefîrtat built animals that stretched his imagination: giants, odd-looking and strange beasts.

In the beginning, everything and everyone seemed to get along together just fine. However, over time evil oozed into these life forms and started wreaking havoc. The tension between these beings is why we still have evil today.

Celtic people

Over nearly 400,000 years, Britain was visited on and off by many hominid species, including the Neanderthal, that had access via land bridges with Europe when the climate permitted. But Homo Sapiens (modern humans) didn't make it to Britain until 40,000 years ago.

Although Celtic culture dates as far back as 3100 years, its exact origin is unknown. The Celts were a group of tribes spread right across Europe and were known for migrating. Over the years, they resided in Turkey, France, Ireland, Britain, Scotland, Wales, and many more places.

Celtic creation story

In the beginning, nothing existed except for the sea and the land. When the sea and land met, the white mare Eiocha was created. On the land, a sturdy and robust oak grew. With seeds from the foam tears of the sea, another plant was formed. Eiocha needed to eat these seeds to live, so these seeds became white berries inside Eiocha. This made Eiocha give birth to the first god, Cernunnos.

Eiocha's childbirth was so painful, she ripped off bark from the oak tree and threw it into the sea. The bark, transformed by the sea, soon became the giants of the deep.

Cernunnos was lonely. Eiocha was pregnant again and gave birth to the gods and goddesses Maponos Tauranis, Teutates and Epona. Eiocha, being made from the sea, grew tired of the land, and returned to her natural home and became the goddess of the deep water, Tethra, also known as Tethys.

The gods and goddesses grew lonely and bored with no one to worship them, so they decided to make the creatures from the oak tree – from there, the first man and woman were created.

Cernunnos also made other creatures – deers, hounds, boar, ravens, hares, and snakes. Because of this, Cernunnos became the god of the animals. He commanded the oak tree to become a forest, a home for all these animals.

Epona made animals in Eiocha's liking – horses, mares, and stallions. From bows, Teutates made arrows and a club from the tree. Tauranis also tried but made thunderbolts of fire and noise instead. From time to time, Tauranis would jump to the tallest of the trees and hurl thunderbolts at the ground. This made the ground shake, the grass burn, and the animals run in fear. The god Manopos, on the other hand, made a harp from the tree. He spends his days playing the harp and the winds.

The sea giants saw the gods and goddesses were happy on their land. This made them jealous as they had no one to worship them. The giants decided to take revenge against the gods. They wanted to flood the land with the sea, taking it underwater. Tethra, however, heard the giants in the waves and warned her children. When the giants launched their attack, the gods were ready.

The gods waited by the oak tree. Tauranis used his thunderbolt, splitting the land, so the sea overflowed at its boundaries. Maponos used the sky against the giants. Teutates used his bow and arrow to strike them down. Although the giants had no weapons, they had the strength of the waves. The gods finally defeated the giants, but they could not destroy them.

When the giants were driven back to the sea, Tethra bound them there. But a few managed to flee Tethra. They made a new civilization on the outer edges of the world and called themselves the Fomor. The

Fomor, however, wanted revenge against the gods. But the day when the Fomor wins still has to come.

After repairing the sea and the sky, the gods then looked for Epona, the only one absent from the battle. Epona had rescued one man and a woman from the battle, and the three waited in Carnunnos' forest. This man and woman would then populate the entire human race. Later the gods returned to their home – the oak tree.

Sami people

Sami people, the descendants of nomadic peoples, had inhabited northern Scandinavia for thousands of years. Sami culture is the oldest in large areas of northern Europe, before the Swedish, Finnish, or even the Viking culture had developed.

Where they came from is obscure. Some think they were Paleo-Siberian, while others maintain that they were alpine and came from central Europe. These indigenous people of northern Europe now live in
 northern parts of Sweden, Norway, Finland, and the Kola Peninsula of Russia. The traditional Sámi lifestyle was dominated until recently by hunting, fishing and trading. For many important environmental, cultural, traditional, and even political reasons, reindeer herding is now legally reserved only *for* Sami people in some Nordic countries.

Sámi creation story

In the beginning, there was only the Sun and the Earth.

The Sun set out on a boat to the land of the Giants to find a wife. There, he fell in love with the Earth, daughter of the blind Giant King.

With the help of this daughter, he won a game of finger pulling against her father, the giant King and earned the right to marry her. As they were once sailing, they were pursued by her angry brothers, who wanted her back.

The couple defeated the brothers with the daughter's magical handkerchief and the Sun's hot rays, burning the brothers to death. They were then married, and she soon gave birth to the ancestors of the Sámi, the Gállá-bártnit. He passed hunting knowledge down to the Sámi.

The Sun and the Earth also had a daughter. Sámi people believe she came to earth to live with the Sámi. She gave the Sámi their reindeer to herd and to look after them.

When she was on her deathbed, she talked about wanting to see her father, the Sun, again. Because the winter darkness was coming in, and she was worried for the Sámi people.

The Nordic region

The Nordic region consists of Denmark, Finland, Iceland, Norway, and Sweden, Faroe Islands and Greenland and Åland. Evidence suggests that modern humans (Homo Sapiens) first arrived in this region sometime between 12,000 and 7000 years ago. Other parts of Europe were already populated at this time.

Norse creation story

Before the dawn of time and before the world was created, there was only a big dark vast emptiness called Ginnungagap. From this, two realms came into existence, Niflheim and Muspelheim. In the north was Niflheim, where it became such a dark and cold place that there was nothing but ice, frost, and fog. Muspelheim was in the south, which became the land of fire. It was so hot that it consisted only fire, lava, and smoke.

Fire giant Surtr lived there along with other fire demons and fire giants.   From the spring called Hvergelmir is all the cold rivers are from. These cold rivers are called Élivágar, meaning ice waves. Each of these many rivers has a name, but as a whole, they are referred to as Élivágar. The water from Élivágar floated down the mountains to the great void, Ginnungagap. It solidified frost and ice, which gradually formed a very dense layer, and grew in size in all directions.

In the middle of Ginnungagap, the air from Niflheim and Muspelheim met. The fire melted the ice and began to drip. Some of the ice started to take the shape of a human-like creature. It was a Jötunn, a giant named Ymir, the first giant in Norse land.

When Ymir fell asleep, he started to sweat. From the sweat under his armpits grew two more giants, one male and one female. His legs paired with each other to create a third, a son, Thrudgelmir "Strength Yeller". These were the first in the family of frost giants, also called Jötnar. They were breastfed by the cow giant Audhumbla, who, like Ymir, was created from the melting ice in Ginnungagap.

The giant cow Audhumbla fed herself on a block of salty ice, and while she was licking on the ice, something strange happened. On the first day, some human hair emerged from the ice. On the second day, Audhumbla again licked on the salty ice, and a head appeared. At last, on the third day, the rest of the body came out. The man who had grown out of the salty rock was Buri, the first of the Gods. Buri was a giant, big and handsome. He later had a son called Borr with his wife, Bestla. They had three more sons, Odin, Vili, and Ve.

Ymir was a frost-giant but not a god, and eventually, he turned to evil. Odin and his two brothers were bothered, and the only solution was to kill Ymir. The three brothers waited until Ymir was asleep before attacking him. In a fierce battle, using all their strength, the brothers managed to kill Ymir. The blood spouted out with a furious force in every direction from Ymir's body, and the other giants drowned in the vast flood of blood.

The world was created from the remains of the giant Ymir. The three brothers dragged Ymir's lifeless body towards the centre of Ginnungagap, and there they created the world from the remains of Ymir. The blood became the oceans, rivers, and lakes. The flesh became the land, and the bones became the mountains. came the land, and the bones became the mountains.

Ymir's teeth were made into rocks, and the hair became the grass and trees. The eyelashes became Midgard. They threw the brain up in the air, and it became the clouds. Ymir's skull turned into the sky like a lid covering the new world. The brothers grabbed some of the sparks shooting out from Muspelheim, the land of fire. They threw the sparks up toward the skull. These sparks became the stars and gleamed at night. On the plains of Idavoll, they built Asgard, which would be the home of the Gods. Very far away from Asgard, in a place called Jotunheim, the giants were allowed to live.

While Odin and his brothers were creating a new world from the body parts of the giant Ymir, worms kept crawling out of the rotting remains, which became the dwarves. The three brothers Odin, Vili, and Ve were afraid that the sky would fall down. They sent out four dwarves in each direction of the world and told them to hold up the sky. The names of the four dwarves are North "Nordi", West "Vestri", South "Sundri", and East "Austri". The rest of the dwarves made their homes in rocks and caves underground, called Svartalheim. They became experts in craftsmanship and created some of the most powerful and magical weapons, like Mjölnir, Thor's hammer. But they also made beautiful jewellery.

The first humans: While walking on the beach, Odin and his two brothers Vili and Vé, found two logs. One was from an ash tree, and the other from an Elm tree. Odin gave the logs spirit and life, and Ve gave them movement, mind and intelligence. Vili gave them shape, speech, feelings, and the five senses. Thus, the first two humans were created. The man was named Ask, and the woman, the name Embla. The Aesir decided the humans should live in Midgard.

Midgard is situated halfway between Niflheim on the north, the land of ice, and Muspelheim to the south, the region of fire. Midgard is joined with Asgard, the abode of the deities, by Bifrost, the rainbow bridge. A man named Mundilfa in ancient times Midgard had two children. They were so shiny and beautiful tha he decided to call his son Mani "Moon" and his daughter Sol "Sun".

The Gods were so furious by this arrogance that they took both of them and pu them up in the sky. Sol rides in a chariot pulled over the sky by two horses Árvak

"Early awake" and Alsviðr, " Very quick". Under the chariot, a shield called Svalin protects the earth below from Sol's flames. Mani is pulled by only one horse, Aldsvider. Mani soon stole two children, Bil and Yuki from Midgard to help him drive his chariot. They are pursued by two wolves, Sköll (Treachery) and Hati (Hate). Hati takes a small bite out of the Moon each day, but the Moon gets away and heals itself again. These two wolves will one day catch the sun and the moon, which will happen at Ragnarök.

Greenland

The first humans arrived in the Arctic region of the Americas arrived about 6,000 years ago, crossing the Bering Strait from Siberia. The Saqqaq people were among the first to arrive in Greenland from present-day Canada around 4,500 years ago.

Sedna is the Mother of the Sea and marine animals in Inuit, also known as Eskimos (culturally similar indigenous peoples living in the Arctic regions of Greenland, Canada, and Alaska) mythology.

Sedna, the Mother of the sea

Sedna was a beautiful maiden who rejected marriage proposals from the hunters of her village. After many refusals, when an unknown hunter appeared, Sedna's father agreed to give her to him as a wife in return for fish. Sedna's father gave Sedna a sleeping potion. Then, he gave her away, almost unconscious, to the hunter. The hunter took her to a large nest on a cliff by the sea and revealed its true form: a great bird spirit (raven). Sedna woke up surrounded by birds.

In the meantime, her father feeling guilty, attempted to rescue her. He came by a kayak next to the cliff. But the bird spirit became angry, causing a great storm. Sedna's father managed to climb the cliff, pulled Sedna out in desperation before throwing her into the raging sea next to his anchored kayak. Trying to cling to her father's kayak, Sedna's hands froze in the iced water, and her fingers fell off. Her fingers became the creatures of the sea, the seals, walruses, and whales. Sedna fell to the bottom of the sea and grew a fishtail and became the Mother of the Sea.

As the patron of all sea creatures, Sedna is the provider of food for the Inuit people. At one time, fishermen became greedy and were unnecessarily killing animals more than they needed. Sea Mother became angry. She sheltered all the creatures in her wild curly hair and dived under the sea to punish the Inuits.

Inuits depended mainly on the catches from the sea for their food. With no catch, everyone was starving. After a few days, under the guidance of a shaman, all of them gathered by the seashore. They promised Sea Mother not to be cruel to animals and kill unnecessarily except for what they needed to survive. Only then did Sea Mother release the creatures from her hair into the sea.

When an Inuit breaks a rule in society, the Mother of the Sea's hair gets filthy. She entangles the animals, preventing the hunters from catching any food. The shaman must then travel over the horizon to the bottom of the ocean to clean her hair and release the animals. He must talk with her to find out which taboos were broken and communicate these lessons back to society.

Northern lights myths

Humans have been fascinated by the waxing and waning of auroral lights from prehistoric times, the closest and most dramatic manifestation of space phenomena. Over the arctic circle, the Northern Light is known as Aurora borealis. Its southern counterpart over the Antarctic circle is known as the Aurora australis. The oldest known auroral citing was written 4700 years ago in China, and 500 years back, Italian astronomer Galileo Galilei coined the term "aurora borealis" after Aurora, the Roman goddess of morning. He thought wrongly that the auroras were due to sunlight reflecting from the atmosphere.

Now it is agreed that Auroras are created when charged particles from the Sun are trapped in Earth's magnetic environment, the magnetosphere, and are funnelled into Earth's upper atmosphere, where collisions cause hydrogen, oxygen, and nitrogen atoms and molecules to glow.

A special type of aurora draped east-west across the night sky, looking like a glowing pearl necklace from spacecraft, is helping scientists better understand the science of auroras.

Aurora stories

Dancing over the winter sky, the northern lights create wonder everywhere it is seen. The people of Greenland in ancient times imagined that the northern lights were dancing each time their ancestors played football with a walrus skull in the sky. Life and death were closely connected to them, and death was just a transformation from one world to another.

Sámi people feared and respected the Northern lights in equal measure. The appearance of the Northern Lights was to them a bad omen. They thought it to be the souls of the dead, and you shouldn't talk about the Northern Lights. It was also dangerous to tease them by waving, whistling or singing under them, as they would alert the lights to your presence. If you caught their attention, the lights could reach down and carry you up into the sky. The Northern Lights could even reach down and slice off your head! To this day, many Sámi stay indoors when the Northern Lights are illuminating the sky, just to be on the safe side!

North America

Homo Sapiens arrived in America many thousand years before Christopher Columbus thought he had discovered America in 1492 and called the indigenous people Indians. He thought he had landed in India!

It is now believed a small modern human population, primarily animal hunters, arrived in frozen Beringia from eastern Siberia in Asia during the Last Glacial Maximum. In this period of the last Ice age, between 33,000 and 11,000 years back, humans expanded into the Americas

Beringia is the land and maritime area bounded on the west by Russia and on the east by Canada. It included the Chukchi Sea, the Bering Sea, the Bering Strait, the Chukchi and Kamchatka Peninsulas in Russia, Alaska in the United States and the Yukon in Canada. This migration would have occurred as the American glaciers blocking the way southward melted, but before the bridge was covered by the sea again, about 11,000 years ago. The earliest American settlers were probably Homo sapiens, but extinct groups like Neanderthals and Denisovans can be ruled out.

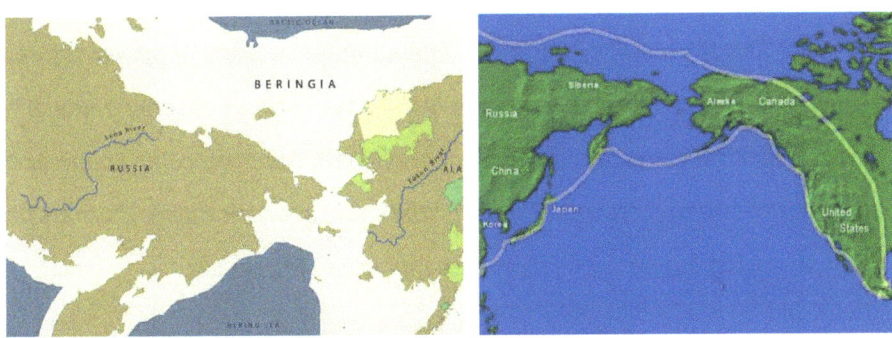

East Asia and America – during the Ice age and now

According to Anthropologists, Ice-Age Paleo-American hunters roamed in North America between 14,000 and 8,000 years back, followed by archaic hunter-gatherers between 8000 and 2000 years ago.

Beaver People

Dane-zaa (meaning those who live among the beaver), often referred to as the Beaver tribe, are a First Nation of the large Athapaskan language group. Their traditional territory is around the Peace River provinces of Alberta and British Columbia, Canada. Recent archaeological evidence established that these areas have been continuously occupied for 10,500 years by varying cultures of indigenous peoples.

The Flood - a tale of the Beaver people

In former times, when people were very numerous upon the earth, once the sun ceased to give heat or light. A continuous fall of snow threatened to annihilate every living creature in the world. The tops of the tallest trees were almost buried in snow, and it was with much difficulty firewood could be obtained.

To find the cause of this awful phenomenon, a party of people agreed to go upon discoveries. After marching many days without observing any difference in the climate, they came upon a squirrel's nest. Squirrels could speak and had great sense and reason. They told the squirrel about their sufferings from the sun having been stolen from them and asked for advice.

The squirrel told them they should wait until he rested and had dreams. After waking from his dream, which lasted a few days, the squirrel said that a she-bear was holding the sun from them.

Some of the beaver people with this information left to search for the bear. They managed the wise squirrel to come with them. After a strenuous walk, they arrived in a beautiful country where the bear with her two cubs lived. The mother bear was out, on the other side of the lake by her den. The beaver people's attention was soon drawn to a long line of Babishe net (untanned animal hide strips used for the lacing) suspended from the cloud and tied to a piece of wood over the bear's den. On this line, at certain distances, were many bags neatly laced with Babishe and containing something mysterious.

While the beaver people were looking at this remarkable net, the wise squirrel said that no time should be wasted, as the mother bear might come back soon. The people should try to find an explanation of the sun's absence by threatening the cubs about the Babishe. Soon the beaver people entered the den with bows and arrows and threatened the cubs with instant death if they did not reveal their mother's secrets. The bear cubs were terrified and agreed to comply.

When asked what the first bag on that Babishe contained, the cubs replied snow. "The second?" Rain, they replied. The third, they said, held thunder and the fourth the Stars. When asked about the fifth bag, the cubs initially refused to answer, but the people held their daggers and arrows to the cubs' chest to frighten them. Very reluctantly, they replied that the fifth bag contained the sun.

Now the wise squirrel commanded to his assistance a pike, a loche (giant slug) and a mouse. The squirrel asked the pike and the loche to quickly get the bag with the sun from the Babishe. The mouse was asked to go to the den's entrance from the lake and nibble through it halfway so that it would break when the mother bear tried to come in.

Off they went upon their errands. The loche was very slow, but the pike soon managed to untie the bag. The pike taunting the slug for being so tardy came down with the pack and started cutting the bag with its teeth. The mouse also came back after doing its task.

But the bear was soon coming back on her canoe from the lake. As she came near, seeing strangers at her home, she quickened her speed on her canoe. With excessive speed, however, the paddle broke. By then, the pike had made a small hole in the bag. To the enormous joy of the beaver people, out of it came the Sun.

The brightness of the sun dazzled and entirely disconcerted the bear. The earth trembled with her howling, and to make her way without her paddle, she thrust herself into the water. She swam and made the best speed she could using her paws. But soon realised that revenge was now out of her power without the sun under her control. By then, the beaver people had already fled.

The adventurer people, on return, however, found themselves plunged into another crisis. Soon, they were threatened with a deluge from the melting of the snow from the sun's heat. The waters increased more and more. The beaver people rapidly ran to get to the summit of a very high rocky mountain.

Unfortunately, only two of them, a man and his wife, reached the top of the mountain. But all the rest were drowned in the waters. On the summit were gathered two of every living creature (male and female) that lived upon the

Earth. Many of the drowned people transformed themselves into birds in the air and remained in the place.

The duck courageously dived into the waters to try to find the ground. But soon came up with nothing and was a laughingstock to his companions. The plongeur, the Dipper who could walk and fly underwater, was next but found nothing. Then the buzzard dived and remained underwater until his strength was almost exhausted but was also unsuccessful.

After a few days, they dived again. But this time, when the buzzard came up, totally exhausted, it had its bill full of earth. This meant that the waters were receding. Gradually the waters dried upon the earth. But as yet, the situation was still deplorable, as they could scarcely find even roots for their subsistence.

During this period, the ducks changed the colour of their feathers (before that time, all were white). Soon after this event, Corbeau (raven) made his appearance. "Come, have a look at my feathers. Are they not beautiful? Don't you not wish to have a coat like mine?" said the duck to Corbeau.

Corbeau was jealous but said, "With your crooked bill, don't you think white suits you better than any other colour?"

The other birds argued with Corbeau, but he was adamant and obnoxious. Exasperated sparrowhawks and the other birds wanted to teach the Corbeau a lesson. They each took a lump of burnt coal in their bills and blackened him all over. Corbeau, enraged at this treatment, and determined not to be the only blackbird, flew upon a flock of starlings (etourneaux). Then it spattered them all over with black. That is why starlings are also black.

Some days afterwards, Corbeau, to annoy his enemies, paid them another visit. This time he brought on his neck a collar with lumps of moose and reindeer fat. The sparrowhawks and the others asked for some of that fat as they were very hungry. Corbeau did not share, nor did he want to tell them where he found the fat. All the birds were furious and decided to rob him. The sparrowhawks were pitched for this job. Soon with one grub each, they carried off all the fat. Corbeau wanted to chase them but thought the better of it as all the birds were against him. He felt fortunate not to have been hurt.

But, after finding the fat with the Corbeau, other birds wanted to find its source. The chouette (the owl) agreed to observe Corbeau in his flight. The owl told the sparrowhawk to throw some ashes upon his own eyes. This allowed the owl to follow without blinking and was able to follow Corbeau to his retreat in a valley beyond a very high mountain.

As soon as this fortunate discovery was made, both men and the animals were informed. The next day, they all decided to go in search of Corbeau's dwelling. Already suffering from lack of food and the fatigue of the journey, they arrived at Corbeau's retreat. It was a lodge covered with the branches of the fir tree. The door was made of reindeer hide. The wolf offered to break open the door. But the fox, because of his known cunning and swiftness, was given this job. The fox, running with all his strength, split open the door. There was a vast number of moose and reindeer prisoned in this lodge, and they were freed.

The man with his wife with their children killed only some of these animals. Once they had enough provisions for a long time, they let the rest go unhurt as they pleased. They agreed with the beasts of the earth and the birds to retain everyone in their present form, breed and cover the earth. They agreed to wander anywhere each chose and not to change into any other form and likeness. This separation continues to this day.

Iroquois

The Iroquois or Haudenosaunee (People of the Longhouse) are indigenous people in northeast North America.

Each village had its own storyteller who was responsible for learning all the stories by heart. No stories were ever told during the summer months. Violations would be punished by the Jo-ga-oh, the "Little People" (like fairies), invisible nature spirits. If the violator ignored the warning, he would suffer greater evils.

Haudenosaunee creation story

The Haudenosaunee have always recognized that people are complex, possessing both good and bad qualities. The Creation story serves as a reminder: no human is flawless– the Great Spirit alone is perfect. This is a story told to children and grandchildren by their parents and grandparents over many generations. It is about the birth of the Evil Spirit and the Good Spirit.

Long, long ago, the earth was deep beneath the water. There was great darkness because no sun or moon or stars shone. The only creatures living in this dark world were water animals such as the beaver, muskrat, duck, and loon, the diver bird.

Far above the water-covered earth was the Land of the Happy Spirits, where the Great Spirit lived. A giant apple tree with roots that sank deep into the ground was in the centre of this upper realm.

One day the Great Spirit pulled the tree up with its roots creating a big pit in the ground. The Great Spirit called to his daughter, who lived in the Upper World. He commanded her to investigate the pit. She did as told, and peered through the hole. In the distance, she saw the Lower World covered by water and clouds.

The Great Spirit asked his daughter Ata-en-sic, who was pregnant, to go into the world of darkness. He tenderly picked her up and dropped her into the hole. The woman began to slowly float downward and was called Sky Woman by those watching her fall.

As Sky Woman came down, the water animals looked up. Far above them, they saw a great light that was Sky Woman. The animals were scared in the beginning because of the light coming out of her. In their fear, they dove deep under the water. But the animals eventually conquered their fear and came back up to the surface. They were then worried about the woman and what would happen to her when she reached the water.

The beaver told the others that they must find a dry place for her to rest upon. The beaver plunged deep beneath the water in search of earth. He was unsuccessful. After a time, his dead body surfaced to the top of the water. Loon, the diver bird, was the next to try to find some earth. He, too, was unsuccessful. Many others tried, but each animal failed.

At last, the muskrat said he would try. When his dead body floated to the top, his little claws were clenched tight. The others opened his claws and found a little bit of earth. The water animals summoned a great turtle and patted the soil upon its back. At once, the turtle grew and grew, as did the amount of earth. This earth became North America, a great island.

During all this time, Sky Woman had continued her gentle fall. The leader of the swans grew concerned as Sky Woman's approach grew imminent. He gathered a flock of swans that flew upward and allowed Sky Woman to rest upon their backs. With great care, they gently placed her upon the newly formed earth.

Soon after her arrival, Sky Woman gave birth to twins. The firstborn became known as the Good Spirit. The other twin caused his mother much pain, and Sky Woman died during his birth. He was known as the Evil Spirit. The Good Spirit took his mother's head and hung it in the sky, and it became the Sun. The Good Spirit also fashioned the stars and moon from his mother's body. He buried the remaining parts of Sky Woman under the earth. Thus, living things may always find nourishment from the soil, for it springs from Mother Earth.

While the Good Spirit provided light, the Evil Spirit created darkness. The

Good Spirit created many things, but his evil brother attempted to undo his good work each time. The Good Spirit made the tall and beautiful trees, including the pines and hemlock. The Evil Spirit, to be contrary, stunted some trees or put gnarls and knots in their trunks. Other trees he covered in thorns or poisoned their fruit.

The Good Spirit made bear and deer. The Evil Spirit made poisonous animals such as lizards and serpents to destroy the animals created by his brother. When the Good Spirit made springs and streams of pure crystal water, the Evil Spirit poisoned some and placed snakes in others. The Good Spirit made beautiful rivers. The Evil Spirit pushed rocks and dirt into the rivers creating swift and dangerous currents.

Everything the Good Spirit made his wicked brother attempted to destroy. After the Good Spirit completed the earth, he created man out of red clay. Placing the man upon the earth, the Good Spirit instructed the man about how he should live. The Evil Spirit made a monkey from sea foam.

After finishing his work, the Good Spirit granted a protecting spirit upon all his creations. Then he called his brother and told him he must stop making trouble. The Evil Spirit flatly refused. The Good Spirit became angry at his brother's wickedness and challenged his evil twin to a fight. The winner would become the ruler of the world.

For their weapons, they used the thorns of the giant apple tree. The battle raged for many days. The Good Spirit triumphed, overcoming his evil brother.

The Good Spirit took his place as ruler of the earth and banished his brother to a dark cave under the ground. The Evil Spirit, however, has wicked servants who do his bidding and roam upon the earth. The wicked spirits can take any form and cause men to do evil things.

This is the reason that everyone has both a good heart and an evil heart. Regardless of how good a man is, he still possesses some evil. The reverse also is true. And however bad a man may be, he still has some good qualities. No man is perfect.

The Good Spirit continues to create and protect mankind. It is the Good Spirit who controls the spirits of good men upon their death. His wicked brother takes possession of the souls of those who are evil like himself. And so, it remains.

Blackfoot people

Once referred to as "Lord of the Plains", the Blackfoot or Siksika people were among the most feared and respected warrior nations in North America. They dominated the plains from the Rockies to Saskatchewan. With the assistance of dogs and later horses, the Blackfoot followed the herds of buffalo for sustenance. They shared stories and traditions reflecting their vast knowledge of the land, sky, plants, and animals. This knowledge helped them thrive for thousands of years on North America's prairies.

Their name came from the colour of their soft animal leather shoes. Siksikas traditionally painted the soles of their moccasins black. However, one legend claimed that the Siksika walked through ashes of prairie fires, which coloured the bottoms of their shoes black.

Head War Chief, Stu-mick-o-súcks (Buffalo Bull's Back Fat) by George Catlin

Sun and the Moon

Once, a family of a man, wife, and two sons lived off berries and other food they could gather, as they had no bows and arrows or other tools. The man had a dream: he was told by the Creator Napi to get a large

spider web and put it on the trail where the animals roamed. Then they would get caught up and could be easily killed with the stone axe he had. The man did so and found it worked.

One day, he came home from bringing in some fresh meat from the trail and found his wife was putting on some perfume on herself. He thought that she must have another lover since she had never done this before. He then told his wife that he was going to get another spider web and asked her to bring in the meat and wood he had on the trail from his hunt. She reluctantly went out and passed over a hill. The wife looked back three times and saw her husband in the same place she had left him, so she continued her walk to retrieve the meat.

The man then asked his children if they knew the place where their mother went to find wood. They knew the area. The man set out and found the timber next to a den of rattlesnakes, one of which was his wife's lover. He set the wood on fire and killed the snakes. He knew by doing this that his wife would become angry, so the man returned home. He told the children to flee and gave them a stick, stone, and moss to use if their mother chased after them.

He remained at the house and put a web over his front door. The wife tried to get in but became stuck and had her leg cut off. She then put her head through, and he cut that off too. While the body followed the husband to the creek, her head followed the children. The oldest boy saw the head behind them and threw the stick. The stick turned into a great forest. When the head made it through, the younger brother told the elder to throw the stone. He did so, and where the stone landed, a huge mountain popped up. It spanned from big water (ocean) to big water, and the head was forced to go through it, not around.

The head met a group of rams and said to them she would marry their chief if they butted their way through the mountain. The chief agreed, and they butted until their horns were worn down. Only some ravines and cliffs opened up, but it was still not enough. She then asked the ants if they could burrow through the mountain with the same stipulations. They agreed and got her the rest of the way through.

From far ahead, the children saw the head rolling behind them. The boys wet the moss and wrung it out behind themselves. They were then in a different land. The country they had just left was now surrounded by water. The head rolled into the water and drowned. The children decided to build a raft and head back. Once they returned to their land, they found that it was occupied by the crows and the snakes. So, they decided to split up.

One brother went north and created the Blackfoot people. The other was smart and went south to make white people and taught them valuable skills.

The woman still chases the man: she is the Moon, and he is the Sun. If she ever catches him, it will always be night on the earth.

Abenaki people

The Abenakis call themselves "Alnôbak", meaning "Real People".
The Abenaki (Abnakior *Alnôbak*) are indigenous First Nation people of northeastern North America.

Abenaki creation story and the importance of dreaming

The Great Spirit, in a time unknown to us, looked around and saw nothing. No colour. No beauty. Time was silent in darkness. There was no sound. Nothing could be seen or felt.

The Great Spirit decided to fill this space with light and life. With his great power, he commanded the spark of creation. He ordered the Great turtle To'lba to come from the waters and become land. The Great Spirit then moulded the mountains and the valleys on the turtle's back. He put white clouds into the blue sky. He felt pleased and said to himself, 'Everything is ready now. I will fill this place with happy movements of life.'

He went on thinking about what kind of creatures he would create. Where would they live? What would they do? What would their purpose be? He wanted it to be a perfect plan. He thought so hard that he became exhausted and fell asleep. His sleep was filled with dreams of his creations. He saw strange things in his dreams. Animals were crawling on four legs, some on two. Some creatures flew with wings, and others swam with fins. There were plants everywhere of all colours. Insects buzzed, dogs barked, birds sang, and humans on two legs called each other.

Everything seemed out of place. The Great Spirit thought he was having a bad dream. He thought nothing could be so chaotic and imperfect. But when the Great spirit woke up, he saw a beaver nibbling on a branch. He realised that the world of his dream had become his creation. Everything he dreamt about had come true. He was still not sure about how good his creation was. Then he saw the beaver make a dam from the branches it gnawed to make a home for his family to swim and a nest for its babies to grow up. The Great Spirit then knew that everything has its place and purpose for the years to come. He was happy.

Abenaki people have told this story from generation to generation – we must not question our dream. They are our creations.

Cree people

The Cree are North American indigenous people. They live primarily in Canada, where they form one of that country's largest First Nations.

Cree creation story - The Origin of the Moon

A *long time ago, there was no moon. There was only the sun.*

The Creator had caretakers. One of them was the Sun, who had two children. One was a boy and the other a girl. Three of them lived happily in the sky. The daughter looked after their place and always kept it clean and tidy. When she shook the beddings, made of feathers, the feathers would sometimes fall to the earth as snow. The son hunted and went fishing. When he hung his nets to dry, droplets from them fell to the world as rain. His job was also to keep a great fire burning in the sun.

When the father became old, one day, the fire was low on the sun. The father came home looking very tired. He said, "Children, my dear children. I have to go, and I will never return".

Before leaving, he gathered them and said, "When I die, you must keep the fire burning. Otherwise, the people and animals on the earth will die".

The children cried and mourned as they knew he would be dying.

The next morning, it was time to start the sun's fire. The children began to quarrel over who should do the job. The sister, after a while, said, "Don't bother. I will start the fire. I am the sister". This hurt the brother's ego, and he said, "No, I am the man. I will do it". They started yelling at each other.

Soon the people on the earth began to worry, saying, "why is the sun so late? It should be up by now!"

Wisakecahk went to the sun to see what was happening. When he arrived, the brother and his sister were still arguing. Wisakecahk became angry. "The people and the animals will perish without the sun", he said to them "it is your job to keep the fire burning!" He told the boy, "your name from now will be Pisim". To the sister, he said, "from now on, you too have to work hard as your brother. You will keep the fire in another place. You will work at night. You will be called Tipskawipism, the moon. As a punishment, you will see each other only once a year. At other times you will only see each other across the sky. And so, it happened. Even now, it is so.

Wisakecahk is one of the most famous Cree heroes. Stories about Wisakecahk always have a moral, and the storyteller may add characters from another story or change the story to make a certain point. Wisakecahk has many powers, such as changing shape and being anything he wishes, speaking the languages of animals and plants. No one really knows what he really looks like.

Grandmother teaches the lazy boy a lesson

When Elder Brother was young, he was greedy, lazy, and didn't want to do what he was told. So, the animals, all of Creation, met one day, and they decided they wouldn't help him anymore and just shunned him. He was starving when he woke up. Because he was lazy, he hadn't combed his hair, he hadn't cleaned himself but started walking, thinking somebody would give him duck soup or something to eat.

But nobody gave him any food, nobody helped him with anything, and nobody talked to him. So, by the end of the day, he was starving and didn't understand why nobody helped. He came to a fire, where Grandmother was cooking lunch. This was the First Grandmother, and she was the first female on the earth.

When she went out, he looked at the food and thought, "she's very old and won't know if I eat these. She will think they fell in the fire and burned." So, he grabbed the little ducks she had roasting over the fire and gobbled them all up really quickly. Then he took the leftover bones and skin and stuck them in the ashes. He messed up in a way to look as if these little ducks had fallen in the fire.

Then he went and laid down under a big tree. Laying there looking at the clouds, he thought about what he would do the next day like the lazy people do, lying around and dreaming about the next day. Then he fell to sleep.

In the meantime, First Grandmother has gone out in the bush picking some medicinal berries. She had a great gift of sight and hearing. She knew what he had done. She said to herself: "that's it, I'm going to teach him a lesson". So, she sang a song which went over the trees. It moved around and found him lying under a tree. The song entered him. She sang the song with higher and higher notes. The higher she went with the notes, the more his stomach swelled up. Finally, his stomach was hurting so much that he stood up.

Little chickadee birds were sitting upon the tree branches and watching all this. Chickadees are like the newscasters in the forest. They were reporting back on all his actions to all in the woods. The lazy man got up, but his stomach was hurting so much, he said: "I have to do something. I don't know what's wrong with me."

At that point, First Grandmother hit a really high note. It made the lazy man blew a great big boikedo (fart). It was the first fart in all Creation; nobody had ever heard one before. And these poor little chickadees were so frightened they almost fell off the branches. And the smell was so horrible they had to fly away. The lazy man could not stop farting because the First Grandmother kept singing.

He staggered, trying to walk home, but he just farted little ones, big ones, and all kinds. He could not stop. Finally, he told his bum that he was going to punish it if it didn't stop. But it didn't stop, so he went and sat on the fire to punish his bum.

And the story goes on and on from there. It takes many days to tell. We'd have to come back tomorrow and help our granny again so that we'd get the rest of the story. You know when you're a little girl or a little boy, and you hear that from the time you were little, for sure you're not greedy and try to take any of the old people's food or anybody else's. Because you could end up like Elder Brother.

And the stories were so funny, but you also knew that they could be true, especially when you'd heard somebody making all kinds of rude noises. So those stories had all of these little lessons, but they also told us at the same time the role of those little birds in Creation and how we should treat them with respect because they had a role in their territory. The word "fart" is "boikedo", which is kind of like "big wind." And we would all just roll around laughing, which made it even worse when you lay in bed, and you'd think about your mother telling you to comb your hair, and you didn't. Everybody is just going to kill themselves laughing when they hear you.

Those remarkable stories were told to children to instil values and manners, taboos, and all those kinds of things in our minds. And when you heard them over and over again, you grew up, and you knew that you shouldn't be dirty and that you shouldn't be greedy, you know, you shouldn't be dishonest.

Each village had its own storyteller who was responsible for learning all the stories by heart. No stories were ever told during the summer months. Violations would be punished by the Jo-ga-oh (little people - invisible nature spirits, similar to the fairies). If the violator ignored the warning, he would suffer greater evils.

Navazo people

The term Navajo comes from Spanish missionaries who referred to the Pueblo Indians through this term, although they called themselves the Diné, meaning 'the people'. Navazos are Native American people of the Southwestern United States and is the largest indigenous tribe in the United States.

The Navajos speak a Na-Dené Southern Athabaskan language called Diné bizaad, meaning 'People's language'. It is now believed that they came from western Canada to southern Arizona and New Mexico some one thousand years ago.

The Age of Beginning

The First World, Ni'hodilqil, was black as black wool. It had four corners, and over these appeared four clouds which were black, white, blue, and yellow. These four clouds contained within themselves the elements of the First World.

The Black Cloud represented the Female Being. As a child sleeps while being nursed by a mother, life rested in the darkness of the Female Being. The White Cloud represented the Male Being. He was the Dawn, the Light which awakens, of the First World. The First World was small, an island floating in the mist. On it grew one tree, a pine tree, which was later brought to the present world for firewood.

In the East, where the Black Cloud and the White Cloud met, the First Man [spirit] was formed. Along with him was made the white corn, perfect in shape, with kernels covering the whole ear. In the West, where the Blue Cloud and Yellow Cloud met, the First Woman [spirit] was formed. With her was created the yellow corn, which was also perfect. With the First Woman came the white shell, turquoise, and evergreen yucca plant with tough, sword-shaped leaves and white.

First Man, the Life-Giver, representing the Dawn, stood on the eastern side of the First World. Opposite in the West stood the First Woman, representing Darkness and Death. First Man burned a crystal for a fire. The crystal was the symbol of the mind and of clear seeing. First Woman burned her turquoise for a fire. They saw each other's lights in the distance, and each went to see the other's fire.

When the First Woman came to him, the First Man said to her, "Why don't you come with your fire, and we will live together?"

The woman agreed. So instead of the man going to the woman, the woman went to him, as is the custom now. About this time, another being, the Great Coyote, formed in the water in the form of a male being. He told the two that he had been hatched from an egg. He knew about all that was under the water and all that was in the skies. First Man placed the Great Coyote ahead of himself in all things. The three began to plan what was to come next.

   While they were busy discussing, another being came to them. He had the shape of a man, wore a hairy coat, lined with white fur, that fell to his knees and was belted in at the waist. His name was Atse'hashke', the coyote called First Angry. He said to the three: "You believe you were the first beings, but you are mistaken. I was already living when you were made."

   Then four other beings came together. They were yellow in colour and were called the tsts'na, the wasps. They knew the secret of shooting evil and could harm others. They were very powerful. After the wasps came the tiny spider ants with their red shirts and little black eyes and a whole crowd of black ants who also knew the secret of shooting evil and were powerful. After many of the wasps and ants came Spider Man and Woman and the Salt Man and Woman.

Ni'hodilhił
First World

   By this time there were many people. The people, however, were not in their present form. The male and female creatures of the First World were Mist People. They had no definite shape but later changed to humans, beasts, and birds. The First World, being small, became crowded. The people quarrelled and fought among themselves, and in every way, living became very unhappy.

The Second World formed because of the strife in the First World. First Man, First Woman, the Great-Coyote, the Coyote called First-Angry and all others followed by climbing up from the Water of Darkness and Dampness to the Second or Blue World. They found several people already living there: bluebirds, blue hawks, blue jays, blue herons, and all the blue-feathered beings. The powerful swallow people lived there too. These people of the Second World did not want those who had come from the First World. There was fighting and killing.

The First Four found an opening in the World of Blue Haze. They climbed through this and led the people up into the Third or Yellow World. The bluebird was the first to reach the Third or Yellow World. After he came the First Four and all the others. A great river, the Female River, crossed this land from north to south. The Male River crossed this river from east to west. The name of this place was the Crossing of the Waters. There were six mountains in the Third World. In the East was Sis na'jin,[Blanca Peak, Colorado], meaning White Shell Mountain. In the South stood Tso'dzil [Mt. Taylor, New Mexico], called the Blue Bead or Turquoise Mountain. In the West stood Dook'oslid, the Abalone Shell Mountain. In the North stood Debe'ntsa, meaning Obsidian Mountain. There were two more sacred mountains: Dzil na'odili, Upper Mountain or centre place, and Chol'i'i.

There was no sun in this land, only the two rivers and the six mountains, and it was a misty place of mountains and rivers. Many people lived in the Third World. Turquoise Boy lived in the east, and a giant male reed grew near him.

White Shell Girl lived in the west, and the giant female reed grew near her. The Agate people, the Seed People, and four holy beings moved to the east, twelve female beings and four more Holy Beings to the west. The ancestors of the Pueblo people also lived in the Third World. On the mountains also lived the turkey people, cat people, snakes, and other animals.

The beaver people lived along the rivers. The frogs and turtles and all the underwater people lived in the water. So far, the people still had no definite shape, but they had different names because of their different characteristics. Now the plan was to bring plants to the world. First Man called the people together. He brought along the white corn which had been formed with him. First Woman got the yellow corn. They laid the perfect ears on the side of the corn next to each other.

Then they asked persons from the gathering to come and help them. Turkey came first. They asked him where he had come from, and he replied that he had come from the Grey Mountain. He danced back and forth four times, then he shook his feather coat and dropped four kernels of corn from his clothing, one grey, one blue, one black, and one red. Next, the Big Snake came forward. He likewise brought four seeds, the pumpkin, watermelon, cantaloupe, and muskmelon. His plants all crawled along the ground as they grew. They planted the seeds and had a plentiful harvest.

But soon, the people began to quarrel. The men blamed the women, and the women blamed the men. After a while, the men decided to move across the river. They thought they could live better separately. But soon, the men began to miss the women, and the women started to miss the men. Even though they could live separately, they didn't like it. Then the people decided to live together again and lead better lives. Some of the women tried to join the men and drowned in the river.

The people moved to different parts of the land. Some time passed. Soon the First Woman became troubled by the monotony of life. She made a plan. She went to Atse'hashke, the Coyote called First Angry and giving

him the rainbow, she said: "I have suffered greatly in the past. I have suffered from wanting meat, corn, and clothing. Many of my maidens have drowned. I have suffered much. Take the rainbow and go to the place where the rivers cross. Bring me the Water Buffalo's two pretty children, a boy and a girl."

The Coyote agreed. He walked over the rainbow. He entered the home of the Water Buffalo and stole the two children. These he hid in his oversized skin coat with the white fir lining. And when he returned, he refused to take off his coat but pulled it around himself and looked very wise. After this happened, people saw a white light in the East and in the South, West, and North. One of the deer people ran to the East and, on return, said that the white light was a great sheet of water. The sparrow hawk flew to the South, the great hawk to the West, and the kingfisher to the North. They returned and said that a flood was coming. The kingfisher said that the water was greatest in the North and that it was near.

The flood was coming, and the Earth was sinking. And all this happened because Coyote had stolen the two children of the Water Buffalo, and only the First Woman and Coyote knew the truth. When the First Man learned of the coming flood, he sent word to all the people and told them to come to the mountain called Sis na'jin. He told them to bring with them seeds of all the plants used for food. All living beings were then to gather on the top of Sis na'jin. First Man travelled to the six sacred mountains, and, gathering earth from them, he put some from each in his medicine bag.

The water rose steadily. When all the people were halfway up Sis na'jin, the First Man discovered he had forgotten his medicine bag. Now, this bag contained not only the earth from the six sacred mountains but his magic, the medicine he used to call the rain down upon the earth and to make things grow. He could not live without his medicine bag, and he wanted to

jump into the rising water. But the others begged him not to do this. They went to the kingfisher and asked him to dive into the water and recover the bag. When the kingfisher brought the medicine bag to the First Man, he breathed on it four times and thanked his people. They all gathered on top of Sis na'jin.

The Turquoise Boy had brought the giant male reed, and the white Shell Girl had the giant female reed with her. Another person had poison ivy, and the spider had brought cotton, which was later used for cloth. The First man planted the evergreen spruce on top of Sisna'jin. But this tree did not reach the next world, so the First Man planted the giant male reed. All the people blew on it, and it grew and grew until it reached the canopy of the sky. They tried to blow inside the reed, but it was solid. They asked the woodpecker to drill out the hard heart. Soon, they could peek through the opening, but they had to blow and blow before it was large enough to climb through. They climbed inside the giant male reed, and after them, the water continued to rise.

The people reached the Fourth World but found it was not a very big place. The last person to crawl through the reed was the turkey from Gray Mountain. His feather coat was flecked with foam from the rising water. With the water also came the female Water Buffalo, who pushed her head through the opening in the reed. She had a lot of curly hair which floated on the water, and she had two horns, half black half yellow. From the tips of the horns, lightning flashed. First Man asked the Water Buffalo why she had come and why she had sent the flood. She said nothing. Then the Coyote drew the two babies from his coat and said it was perhaps because of them being stolen.

The Turquoise Boy took a basket and filled it with turquoise. On top of the turquoise, he placed blue pollen from the blue flowers and yellow pollen from the corn. He piled it with the pollen from the water flags [irises], then the crystal, the river pollen. This basket he gave to the Coyote, who put it between the horns of the Water Buffalo. The Coyote said that with this sacred offering, he would give back the male buffalo child.

He said that the male child would be known as the Black Cloud or Male Rain, bringing thunder and lightning. He kept the female child to be known as the Blue, Yellow, and White Clouds or Female Rain. She would be the gentle rain that would moisten the earth and help them to live.

Coyote placed the male child on the sacred basket between the horns of the Water Buffalo. The Water Buffalo disappeared, and the waters retreated with her.

After the water receded, there appeared another person they did not know. They asked him where he had come from. He told them that he was the badger (nahashch'id) and that he was formed where the Yellow Cloud, which was the sunbeam, had touched the Earth.

First Man was not satisfied with the Fourth World. It was a small, barren land, and the great water had soaked the earth and made the sowing of seeds impossible. He planted the giant female reed, and it grew up to the vaulted roof of this Fourth World. First Man sent the newcomer, the badger, up inside the reed, but water began to drip before he reached the upper world. The badger was frightened and came back.

At this time, there came another strange being, the locust. First Man asked him where he was formed, and he replied he had come from the Earth itself. He said it was now his turn to do something, and he offered to climb the reed. The locust made a headband of a bit of reed, and on his forehead, he crossed two arrows. These arrows were dressed in yellow tail feathers. With this sacred headdress, the locust climbed up to the Fifth World. He dug his way through the reed as he digs in the earth even now. He then pushed through the mud of the Fifth World until he came to water.

When he came out, he saw a black waterbird swimming toward him. The waterbird had two arrows crossed at the back of his head and had big eyes. The bird said: "What are you doing here? This is not your country." He told the locust that unless he could make magic, he would not be allowed to stay. The black water bird drew an arrow from the back of his head and, shoving it into his mouth, drew it out at the other end of his body. Then he inserted it underneath his body and drew it out of his mouth.

"That is nothing," said the locust. Taking the arrows from the headband, he pulled them both ways through his body, between his shell and his heart. The bird believed that the locust possessed great power, and he swam away to the East, taking the water with him. Then came the blue water bird from the South, the yellow water bird from the West, and the white water bird from the North, and everything happened as before. The locust performed the magic with his arrows, and when the last water bird had gone, he found himself sitting on land.

The locust returned to the lower world and told the people that the beings above had strong medicine. He had great difficulty getting the best of them.

Now two dark clouds and two white clouds rose, which meant that two nights and two days had passed, for there was still no sun. First Man again sent the badger to the upper world, and he returned covered with mud, terrible mud. The badger still had black feet from the soil. First Man then gathered chips of turquoise, which he offered to the five Chiefs of the Winds who lived in the uppermost world of all. They were pleased with the gift, and they sent down the winds and dried the Fifth World.

First Man and his people saw four dark clouds and four white clouds pass, and then they sent the badger up the reed again. This time when the badger returned, he said he had come out on solid earth. Then the First Man and the First Woman led the people to the Fifth World, which called the many coloured Earth and some the changeable earth. They emerged through a lake surrounded by four mountains. The water bubbles in this lake when anyone goes near it.

After all the people had emerged from the lower worlds, the First Man and the First Woman covered the Mountain Lion with yellow, black, white, and greyish corn and placed him on one side. They covered the Wolf with white tail feathers and put him on the other side. They divided the people into two groups. The first group was told to choose whichever chief they wished. They thought they had chosen the Mountain Lion but found that they had taken the Wolf for their chief. The Mountain Lion became the chief for the other side. The people who had the Mountain Lion as their chief turned out to be the people of the Earth. They were to plant seeds and harvest corn. The followers of the Wolf became the animals and birds; they turned into all the creatures that fly and crawl and run and swim. And after all the beings were divided, and each had his own form, they went their ways.

That is the story of the Four Dark Worlds and the Fifth, the World we live in. Some medicine men tell us that there are two more worlds above us; the first is the World of the Spirits of Living Things, the second is the Place of Melting into One.

Cherokee

Cherokee people are one of the indigenous peoples of the Southeastern parts of the United States. According to tribal history, Cherokee people have existed since time immemorial. Their oral history extends back through the millennia. Cherokee, an Iroquoian-speaking people, may have migrated in late prehistoric times from northern areas around the Great Lakes over thousands of years.

How the World Was Made

The earth is a grand floating island in a sea of water. At each of the four corners, there is a cord hanging down from the sky. The sky is of solid rock. When the world grows old and worn out, the cords will break, and then the earth will sink down into the ocean. Everything will be water again, and all the people will be dead. The Cherokees are scared of this.

A long time ago, when everything was all water, all the animals lived up above in Galun'lati, beyond the stone arch that made the sky. But it was very crowded. All the animals wanted more room. The animals began to wonder what was below the water. At last, Beaver's grandchild, little Water Beetle offered to go and find out. Water Beetle darted in every direction over the surface of the water, but it could find no place to rest.

There was no land at all. Then the Water Beetle dived to the bottom of the water and brought up some soft mud. The mud grew and spread out on every side until it became the island, we call the earth. Afterwards, this earth was fastened to the sky with four cords, but no one remembers who did this.

In the beginning, the earth was flat and soft and wet. The animals were anxious to get down, and they sent out different birds to see if it was yet dry, but there was no place to alight. So, the birds came back to Galun'lati. He sent out Buzzard and told him to go and make the earth ready for them. This was the Great Buzzard, the father of all the buzzards we see now. He flew all over the land, low down near the ground, but it was still soft. He was exhausted by the time he reached the Cherokee country; his wings began to flap and strike the ground. But there was a valley wherever they struck the earth; there was a mountain whenever the wings turned upwards again. When the animals above saw this, they were afraid that the whole world would be mountains, so they called him back. But the Cherokee country remains full of mountains to this day (original home of the Cherokee in North Carolina).

When the earth was dry, the animals came down, but it was still dark. Therefore, they got the sun and set it on a track to go across the island from east to west every day, just overhead. But it was too hot this way. Red Crawfish had his shell scorched a bright red, which spoiled its meat. That's why the Cherokees still do not eat it.

Then the medicine men raised the sun a handbreadth in the air, but it was still too hot. They raised it another time and then another time. At last, they raised it seven handsbreadths so that it was just under the sky arch. Then it was just right, and they left it like that. That is why the medicine men called the high place "the seventh height." Every day since, the sun goes under this arch of the sky and returns at night on the upper side of the arch to its starting place. There is another world under this earth. It is like this one in every way. The animals, the plants, and the people are the same, but the seasons are different. The streams that come down from the mountains are the trails by which one can reach this underworld. The springs at their head are the doorways by which to enter it. But to access the other world, one must fast and then go to the water and have one of the underground people for a guide. We know that the seasons in the underground world are different. Because the water in the spring is always warmer in winter than the air in this world, and in summer, it is cooler.

No one knows who made the first plants and animals. But when they were first created, they were told to keep awake and watch for seven nights, the way men do now when they fast and pray to their medicine. But trying to do this, on the first night, nearly all the animals stayed awake. The next night several of them dropped asleep.

On the third night, even more, fell asleep. At last, on the seventh night, only the owl, the panther, and one or two more were still awake. They were then given the power to see in the dark, go about as if it were day, and kill and eat the birds and animals which sleep during the night.

Even some of the trees went to sleep. Only the cedar, the pine, the spruce, the holly, and the laurel were awake all seven nights. Because of this, they are always green and are also sacred trees. But the other trees, because they did not stay awake, lose their leaves every winter.

After the plants and the animals, men came to the earth. At first, there was only one man and one woman. He hit her with a fish. In seven days, a little child came down to the earth. Then more people came to this world, so rapidly it seemed as though the earth may not be able to hold them all.

Central America

Olmecs

Olmec was the first major Mesoamerican civilization along the Gulf of Mexico to the east of the Tuxtla mountains over 3700 years ago. Olmecs had their roots in the early farming cultures of the Tabasco region, which began between 7200 years 5700 years back. Olmec culture peaked around 3000 years ago and then gradually disappeared 2500 years ago. The decline of their civilization was possibly due to environmental changes involving nearby volcanic activity. Olmec was among the first Mesoamerican complex societies. Their culture influenced many later civilizations, like the Maya and the Aztec. The Olmecs are known for the massive stone heads they carved from a volcanic rock called basalt.

They were highly talented artists, sculptors and engineers. Most of what we know about the Olmec comes from works they created in stone. They also worked with wood: most wooden Olmec sculptures have been lost, but a handful of them survived at the El Manatí site. The Olmecs built aqueducts, laboriously carving massive pieces of stone into identical blocks with a trough on one end. They then lined these blocks up, side by side, to create a channel for water to flow. That's not their only feat of engineering, however. They built a man-made pyramid at La Venta.

Symbols of Olmec writing date back as far as 3000 years ago, suggesting that the Olmec may have had the earliest writing system of the Americas. The long-count calendar used by other civilizations, notably the Maya, may have been an Olmec invention. Unlike the Maya and Aztec cultures, there is no surviving record of Olmec beliefs. Today, we know only by studying Olmec art and inscriptions that did survive and comparing Olmec views to other, later Mesoamerican cultures.

The Feathered Serpent appeared for the first time in Olmec Mythology. Such a deity later appeared throughout most Mesoamerican cultures. In Mayan mythology, the feathered serpent appears as Kukulkan and among the Aztecs, it is called Quetzacoatl.

Olmec Gods

Olmec Gods were many and varied. Some were summoned for healing. Others represented dark powers, and some were mischievous. Religion was an integral part of their culture. The sun was a part of their worship, along with the jaguar, and they believed everyone had an animal spirit. They practised shamanism with rituals to heal the sick.

Olmec Jaguar God: The jaguar was a crucial figure to the Olmec., the shamans of the animal world. It was referred to as a nahual, an animal so closely related to an individual man that if the animal dies, the man will also die. Olmecs also believed in a were-jaguar, the offspring of a feline father and a human mother. These had the combined features of the jaguar and man in varying degrees, with the puffy face of fat human babies and snarling mouths, fangs, and perhaps even claws. To the Olmecs, were-jaguars were the deities of thunder, lightning, and rain.

Many other depictions of an Olmec God were half jaguar, half serpent. Olmecs were a kind of "mother culture" that directly gave rise to all subsequent major civilisations in Central America. They believed the Jaguar was a rain and fertility god. The Jaguar was chosen because, to the Olmecs, it was the most powerful and feared animal. They also believed that the Jaguar was an Avatar of the living and the dead. Olmec men ritually sacrificed blood to the jaguar, wearing masks, danced, and cracked whips to imitate the sound of thunder. They made numerous statues representing were-jaguar men shown with grimacing Jaguar facial features and human bodies. They were believed to be Olmec people who were transforming into the Jaguar. The tortured facial features of these were not intended to show ferocity and aggressiveness but emotional stress beyond endurance.

To them, it was precisely the sort of physically and mentally exhausting crisis - the crossing of the threshold between two worlds, two kinds of reality, such as the crossing over and transformation into the most powerful predator of the rainforest and the Savannah. That is part and practice of Shamanism everywhere

In all, at least ten Olmec Gods have been identified:

First Mother and First Father: The First Mother and First Father are the Creator Couple. All the other later gods were their offspring. The First Mother, the Moon Goddess, was born six years before the First Father, Hun Nal Ye. Also known as the Maize God and the Plumed or Feathered Serpent, the First Father was responsible for overseeing the new creation of the cosmos.

Hunahpu and Xbalanque: These hero twins overcame the forces of death, paving the way for the conception of humans. They are usually shown wearing red and white cloth headbands, a symbol later of Maya rulership. The hero twins were patron gods of writing and had two older brothers who were jealous of these twins. They did everything they could to make their younger brothers' lives difficult. The Hero Twins changed their brothers into monkeys.

The Maize God: Like the Sun God, the Maize God is associated with life and death. He follows the path across the sky, descends into the Underworld, is reborn, and returns to the Sky World. This deity's flattened and elongated forehead is often accentuated by a partly shaved head and eyebrows, leaving patches of hair on the top of his head, like a ripened ear of corn.

Itzam-Yeh: The Celestial Bird, also known as the Serpent Bird and Seven-Macaw, Itzam-Yeh is associated with the world's four corners.

Itzamná: Lord of the Heavens: Itzamná, or Lizard House, is a high-ranking god who was the first shaman and diviner. The word itz means shaman, a person who could open the portals to the spirit world. Kings and shamans contacted Itzamná to plead with him to open the way so sacred nourishment would flow into the world to sustain humanity. He is also the inventor of writing and the patron of learning and the sciences.

The Jaguar Sun God: Almighty God, the Sun dwells in the highest levels of heaven. When he traces the sun's path across the sky in the daytime, his name is Kinich Ahau. When the sun falls into the West Door and enters the Underworld, he becomes the fearsome Jaguar God.

Ix Chel: Lady Rainbow: Wife to the high god Itzamná, she oversees weaving, medicine, and childbirth. Like the First Mother, she is a moon goddess depicted sitting in a moon sign holding a rabbit.

Chac - The Rain God and Cosmic Monster: Chac is a dragon-like monster with a crocodilian head and deer ears. He exists on the perimeter of the cosmos, marking the path between the natural and supernatural worlds. In the creation, Chacs were placed at the four corners of the world. They bring the rains by shedding their blood and also create thunderbolts by hurling down their stone axes.

The Lords of Death: Many gods lived in the Underworld. The Lords of Death are depicted as skeleton people or ugly bloated beings wearing ornaments such as disembodied eyes taken from the dead.

The Witz monster: The Witz monster is the symbol of the living mountain. Images of this creature were placed on temples to transform them into sacred, living mountains. He is depicted with a huge gaping mouth and a stepped cleft in the centre of his forehead. The open mouth was the entry into the mountain.

K'awil: the god of sustenance: K'awil is associated with royal power, which originates with the gods. He often appeared on ceremonial batons clasped by rulers during ritual ceremonies and ascending to the throne.

We may not have any Olmec stories surviving today but imagine the beautiful stories their children heard from their grandparents and parents over many centuries!

Maya

Maya civilization developed in Mexico, Guatemala, Belize, Honduras and El Salvador. Maya regions around 4000 years ago saw the first developments of the earliest villages and agriculture with staple crops like maize, beans, squashes, and chilli peppers. Mayans were using hieroglyphic writing 2400 years back.

Temple of Kukulkan at Chichen Itza, Mexico

The first Maya cities with monumental architecture, including massive temples with elaborate façades, developed between 2800 and 2500 years ago.

Mayan creation story

The myth was written initially in hieroglyphics in the present-day Yucatan and later translated into the alphabet. *Popol Vuh* is a text recounting the mythology and history of the K'iche's, one of the Maya peoples. Throughout the myth, creation is written, mentioning farming, reflecting the importance Mayans placed on raising crops, mainly maize.

In the beginning, there was nothingness. The world consisted of the sky and the sea. The gods resided in either the sky or the ocean and realized the great potential for emptiness. One god from each region, Plumed Serpent from the sky and Hurricane from the sea, came together to create the world. These two great thinkers filled the emptiness through dialogue. Whatever they said was created (this places a twist on the importance of language). To the Mayans, objects arise from what they're called, not as usually something first exists and then is named.

The two gods discussed how the Earth would be sewn with seeds and who would be its provider (reflecting the importance of agriculture in Mayan culture). First, they created the mountains and plant life. However, the lack of sound on the planet bothered the gods, so they created animals to live in the forests. After the animals were constructed, the gods ordered them to identify themselves. The animals could only bark or grunt or howl as they could not speak. Because of this, they could not correctly worship the gods, which proved unsatisfactory to the deities. The two gods decided the animals were to never leave the forests and to be subservient to the greater humans who would soon be created. Animals were told, 'Just accept your service, just let your flesh be eaten.'

Next, Plumed Serpent and Hurricane began experimenting with making humans. The first invention was mud people, but they quickly proved unsatisfactory as they kept falling apart. Their heads wouldn't turn, and their faces were crooked, and they dissolved soon when exposed to water. The gods quickly did away with these mud people and started afresh.

The second experiment created wooden people. This batch of mankind proved somewhat more successful as they could talk. Their bodies were sturdy;

however, their skin was dry and crusty, and they could not move in a coordinated manner. Worst, they had no memory and no emotions.

Because of this, they were unable to properly respect their creators. Furiously Hurricane sent a flood to do away with the failed wooden people. Those who survived the flood suffered as the Hurricane sent monsters to the Earth to destroy them. The first monster, Bloodletter, ripped off their heads. Gouger of Faces plucked out their eyeballs. Crunching Jaguar and tearing Jaguar ripped off the people's limbs and then ate them. Those who survived the monsters' onslaught then suffered as molten pitch rained down on them, pulverizing their bodies to mere dust. The Earth then blackened, and a continuous rainstorm came.

Wild animals broke into the remaining people's homes, where their griddles and pots had already come alive. Terrified, the remaining wood people attempted to run away, but everywhere they went, they were halted. When they went on their roofs, their houses collapsed. When they climbed trees, they were shaken off the trees. When they ran to caves, the entrances shut in their faces. The monkeys are all that remains of the wooden people as monkeys somewhat resemble humans but are mere manikins.

The gods wanted to create a successful race of humans who could worship them properly. Once this respectable line of beings was created, the sun, moon, and stars would become visible. To ensure that this third and final experiment was successful, the gods sent four animals (a fox, a parrot, a coyote, and a crow) to find a location for the creation. Once these animals found a suitable place with a bounty of food, they brought back maize to an old woman to grind up into a grainy paste. Hurricane and Plumed Serpent then moulded the first human beings out of this paste (maize was a staple food in the Mayan diet).

Four humans were initially created. They were known as "mother-fathers" as they represented both the female and male components of the race. These "mother-fathers" were an instant success as they could express themselves and understand the world around them. They explored their world and the skies thoroughly as they possessed great vision that allowed them to see through objects. At first, the gods were pleased with their creation and its thirst for knowledge. But soon, the humans' knowledge rivalled that of the gods. If this were to continue, then the humans would not worship and respect the gods as they should. So, the Hurricane and Plumed Serpent clouded the humans' vision.

The people began to multiply and fill the Earth; however, the sun still had not risen, so the people wandered the Earth ceaselessly in darkness. Tired of waiting, the people began migrating to the east to search for the sun but soon suffered from starvation. The "mother-fathers" then climbed a mountain and prayed to the gods. The gods were moved by the peoples' prayers and sufferings. The sun began to rise, and the people fell to their knees in thanks. In the beginning, the sun's rays were intolerably hot. However, over time the people were able to enjoy the sun's warmth and light. They were soon allowed to farm the land as they wished, growing maize and other necessary crops.

Aztecs

The people of the allied Central Mexican and American city-states between the 12th century and the 15th-century AD Spanish invasion are commonly known as the Aztecs.

Teotihuacan is an ancient Mesoamerican city located 50 km northeast of modern-day Mexico City and was settled as early as 2500 years ago. It was the most powerful and influential city in the region for almost 1000 years. When Aztecs found the place back and named it Teotihuacan (meaning "the place where the gods were created"), it had been abandoned for centuries. Teotihuacan's origins, history, and culture largely remain a mystery.

Pyramid of the Sun at Teotihuacan

Aztecs, a nomadic warrior tribe in northern Mexico, arrived in Mesoamerica about 800 years ago. They became some of the most important and powerful people in Mesoamerica. They ruled a large empire for the next two hundred years until the Spanish colonial invasion in 1521.

The Creation of the Universe

In the beginning, there was nothing, nothing at all. No light, no life, no consciousness, no movement, no breath. At the beginning of time and in the void, the Oldest of Old Gods, Ometeotl, was formed.

It is the nature of things that Ometeotl, Creator of the Universe, was masculine as well as feminine. This is why the Supreme First God created himself-herself because he-she could bear life alone. And so it was that the Oldest of Old Gods began the Creation in the dark emptiness that was nothing. Ometeotl was the first existence to be. This Oldest of Old Gods was, therefore, everything that was. When everything exists in one being, all opposites unite. The Creator is both generators of chaos and a giver of harmony and order. Ometeotl is both spirit and matter, fire and water, black and white, stillness and movement, life and death, creator and destroyer, and the embodiment of good and evil. Because of this, the Oldest of Old Gods is called the God of Duality, where opposites converge in a supreme manifestation of The All.

In the nothingness of the Void, Ometeotl, The First God, created himself-herself, thought himself-herself up, invented himself-herself, to initiate The Beginning. And then generated all that would exist after that. The Giver of life and the one who takes it away, the Oldest God, both create and destroy Ollin, the sacred movement in a continuum, which gives impulse to our world.

Once created, the Supreme God Ometeotl, being both masculine and feminine, spawned four children who became the ministers of Genesis and the creation of our visible, physical and changing world. These children are separate yet the same. For this reason, they are referred to as the four manifestations of one god, Tezcatlipoca, God of the Smoking Mirror.

The four Tezcatlipocas created our world. They then made the gods destined for the preservation of this world. To sustain all natural phenomena and the unchaining of life forms. These four gods, children of Ometeotl, have ever since served as the guardians of humans, administering both awards and punishment and as our guides.

Our ancestors tell us that once they were born, the four Tezcatlipocas existed for six hundred years. Only after this period, they begin their task of The creation. They created water, the god Tlaloc and his goddess, who together embodied the essence of water. Then the Tezcatlipocas created Cipactli. Cipactli is a dragon-serpent that floats in the void of nothingness. Beyond Cipactli's monster body, nothing exists. Our vast and ever-expanding universe and all the other universes beyond are contained within Cipactli.

In Cipactli's incredible body, the gods gave form to our world. Thirteen heavens exist in Cipactli's head. The earth is a great, flat disc in the middle, and nine underworlds go down the length of Cipactli's tail. Cipactli is so enormous that it is almost impossible to imagine. Our entire existence fits inside. It is surrounded by the Celestial Waters, making our world Cem-á-nahuac, which is surrounded by water.

If one turns east from the heart of these lands, toward the rising sun, and walks and walks to the ends of the earth, one reaches the water. If one turns south, beyond the sun's path, and walks to the earth's limit, the journey ends at the water. In the house of the setting sun, in the west, there is also water. Even in the farthest regions of the north, one will eventually reach a great mass of ice.

But the sun battles with the ice, turning it into water. Thus, the ancient mind knew our world as a flat, round disc surrounded by water. Because their ancestors walked all throughout and found it so. This is what legend tells us. This is their truth.

The world is divided into four great quadrants. At the very centre is the navel. Magical things happen at the earth's navel. From this centre, Ometeotl sends forth his-her powerful energy and controls the cosmos and things to come. From this navel, the four quadrants of the earth extend all the way to the horizons, the heavens, and the surrounding celestial sea. Each of the four regions has different characteristics, as each is distinct in its relation to the sun's passage.

At the end of the earth, where the sun sets, the West is the sun's home. This is the White Tezcatlipoca region, also known as Quetzalcoatl, keeper of wisdom and things related to maize. It is the land of experience, wisdom, old age, light, fertility and life.

Quetzalcoatl rules this land and has those qualities. Opposite the region of the setting sun is the East, the land of the Red Tezcatlipoca, also known as Xipe-Totec. If one were to ever reach there, one would find the region dominated by springtime and rebirth. In the East, the seasons are forever changing, the leaves of trees constantly falling, and buds are continually sprouting forth with new life.

The area to the left of the setting sun is the land of the Blue Tezcatlipoca, known as Tonatiuh, the Sun. This god is the God that is eaten because day after day, the Sun descends to the underworld. It falls into the shadows of darkness while the moon and the stars reign. Fighting against the Night, Tonatiuh is weakened and loses energy.

But the nutrients of life's blood spilt in penitence help fortify the Sun to win the battle against the Night. Each dawn, it emerges from the Underworld. It becomes the Eagle of Fire Bolts, a symbol of victory against the treacherous Night.

The land at the end of the earth to the left of the setting sun, the south, is associated with the colour blue because the trajectory of Tonatiuh is a great circular path along the great celestial dome. The region to the right of the setting sun, the North, is the sacred place of the Black Tezcatlipoca, the Lord of the Night Sky. The god Mictlantecuhtli reigns there. This is the bitter cold and fleshless Land of the Dead. When one dies, one goes directly there, and from that land, the dead set out.

And so, the four Tezcatlipocas, sons of Ometeotl, created the four regions of the world in the middle of Cipactli's great monster body. Above our world, Cem-á-nahuac, they then made the heavens that surround our world. These heavens are like a great blue dome of different levels in which the heavenly bodies move.

In the five lowest heavens are the moon's paths, the stars, the sun, Venus, and the comets. They are covered by the heaven in which the Night extends itself, then the heaven of blue. Beyond is the heaven where Tlaloc dominates the Rain and the crashing of the Obsidian Swords. Just below the highest heaven is the most divine region of all the gods. But above all other heavens is Omeyocán, the place of duality and dwelling place of the supreme deity, generator and founder of the universe, Ometeotl. The Creator of All is alone in the highest heaven.

After the four Tezcatlipocas created the earth and heavens, they formed the nine strata of the Underworld, known as Mictlán. These nine hells are located in the tail of Cipactli -the dragon-serpent that makes up our universe in the Void. In the Underworld, the dead journey for four years through the nine levels, during which time they face perilous tests and dangers. If they overcome these challenges, only then do their souls find rest.

Upon dying, humans travel to the Region of the Dead, where the Black Tezcatlipoca releases them for their journey through the Underworld. They encounter a place below the earth in the first level where they find themselves at the edge of a treacherous river. To cross the river, they need the help of a dog, one that is dedicated to doing just this. If they pass the river, they descend to the next level, to the place where the mountains crash. The dead must cross the moving and shaking mountains quickly to not remain trapped as prisoners for eternity.

In this manner, the dead pass through the trials of Mictlán until they come to the lowest level and face the last obstacle, the extension of the Nine Waters. If overcome, they reach the region of rest, and their soul is liberated from physical suffering.

This is how the four Tezcatilpocas created the four regions of the earth, the celestial waters, heaven and hell. The creation of the universe changes with time and culture. This was the knowledge of our ancestors, a colourful canvas that paints the history of our world, brought down to us through poetry, legend and song.

South America

Amazon

The Amazon is the largest rainforest in the world. It covers about 5,500,000 km^2 in Brazil, Peru, Colombia, Bolivia, Ecuador, Guyana, Suriname, and Venezuela.

The Amazon represents over half of the planet's remaining rainforests. It is the largest and most biodiverse tropical rainforest globally, with an estimated 390 billion individual trees of between 30,000 to 50,000 plant species.

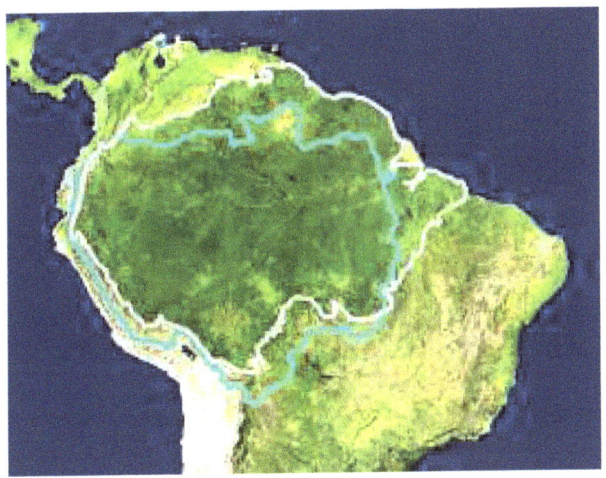

The Amazon watershed covers about 5,846,100 km^2. The mighty Amazon River is crisscrossed by thousands of rivers. This river of between 6,275 and 6,992 km in length has an average discharge of water into the ocean more than the other seven largest independent rivers of the world combined. The Amazon basin is the largest drainage basin globally, with an area of approximately 7,000,000 km^2.

In the Amazon, there are at least 1,400 species of fish, 163 amphibians, 387 reptiles and more than 500 mammals, including 90 primates and 1,300 bird species, of which 20% are endemic and 8.4% are endangered.

Humans have inhabited the Amazon region for nearly 11,000 years. More than 30 million people of 350 different ethnic groups now live in the Amazon, of which 1.6 million are indigenous, belonging to more than 400 tribes, each with its language, culture and territory. The name *Amazon* came after a war European colonists fought with the local tribes. The women fought alongside the men, as was their custom. The name *Amazonas* was derived by the colonists from the Greek mythological word for warrior women.

Amazon – the meeting of the waters. River Negro and River Blanca

Tupi people

The Tupi people were one of the largest indigenous populations in Amazon before European colonisation. They have been living in the Amazon rainforest for nearly 3000 years.

Tupí creation Stories

In Amazon, the myths rely on the animal metaphor as the worldly component of cosmology. In Tupi myth, the Jabuti, the tortoise is the sun, and the Jaguar is the moon. Jabuti is a small species of tortoise, short-legged, slow, and weak.

How Jabuti killed the Jaguar and made a flute out of his bones

A monkey was high up in an Inajá tree eating fruit when a Jabutí came up under the tree and asked, "What are you doing, monkey!"

"I am eating Inajá fruit," the monkey replied.

"Throw one down to me," said the Jabutí.

"Climb up, Jabutí, if you want fruit," sneered the monkey.

"But I cannot climb."

"Then I will come down and fetch you."

Down went the monkey, carried Jabutí up into the tree, and put him on a fruit branch. The monkey later went away, leaving the tortoise, saying that he would come back soon.

Jabutí ate until he was full and waited for the monkey. But a long time went by, and the monkey did not return. He wanted to get down but couldn't. He kept looking towards the ground, scared that he might fall and die.

After a while, a Jaguar came along and, looking up into the tree, saw the Jabutí.

"Hey Jabuti!" he called out, "what are you doing up there?"

"I am eating Inajá fruit".

"Throw me down one!" said the Jaguar.

Jabuti plucked one fruit and threw it to the Jaguar. The Jaguar asked for more, and Jabuti obliged.

"Why don't you come down?" asked the Jaguar.

Jabuti said he was scared that he might die if he fell down. Jaguar now wanted to make a tasty meal out of the tortoise, so he said:

"Don't be afraid! Jump! I will catch you!"

But as Jabuti jumped, he noticed at the last moment the Jaguar had a mischievous grin. He realised that the Jaguar was going to eat him. So Jabuti moved slightly to fall on the Jaguars head and killed him. Jabuti, unhurt, then went off to his hole.

A month later, he came out for a walk. He found the skeleton remains of the Jaguar and carried away one of the bones to his hole. There he made a fife, a high-pitched flute, out of the bone. As he walked about, he played with his fife: "Yauareté kaunguéra sereny'my' '!" The bone of the jaguar is my fife.

Another jaguar, who was passing by, heard the sound. As he listened, "Yauareté kaunguéra sereny'my," Jabuti piped again. Jaguar, worried and curious, followed the tortoise, who had by then reached the mouth of his hole.

"U'l Jabuti!" cried jaguar, "What is that you are saying?"

"What did you say?" asked Jabuti.

"Did I not hear you saying: "Yauareté kaunguéra sereny'my' '!"?

"No," said Jabuti, "I said, "Suasú (the deer) kaunguéra sereny'my'
'!" and immediately he ran into his hole. From there, he piped
gain: "Yauareté kaunguéra sereny'my' '!"

On hearing this, Jaguar turned towards the hole and said: "I am going to eat
you." The Jaguar reached down into the dark burrow and caught hold of the
back end of the Jabuti.

The clever Jabuti shouted out: "Oh, you foolish fellow! You think you have
caught me when it is only the root of a tree that you have got between your
teeth!"

Jaguar released his hold, and Jabuti went deeper into the burrow. Jaguar
waited outside the hole watching for the Jabuti. But he escaped by the other
end of the hole, eluding the Jaguar. A monkey in a tree, seeing the Jaguar
waiting, asked what he was doing.

Jaguar answered: "I am waiting for the Jabutí to come out that I may eat
him."

The monkey laughed and said: "You are stupid. Jabutí has gone away. He will
not come back."

In this myth, Jabutí is the sun who conquers and kills the Jaguar moon. The
moon Jaguar chases the sun Jabutí, who enters his burrow by one hole and
escapes by another. Just as the sun disappears from the earth in the west and
comes up out of the east. Taking the bones for making a fife was also easy for
Tupi children to understand as flutes were usually made from animal bones.

In the present day, two South American countries have indigenous peoples with the largest ethnic groups. In Peru, 45% are indigenous, and in Bolivia, 62% identify as part of some indigenous group.

Aymara and Quechua

The Aymara and Quechua are indigenous people in the Andes and Altiplano regions of South America. Aymara and Quechua people share many cultural attributes and practices, such as their belief in Pachamama, an Andean deity ('Earth Mother').

Quechua people speak the Quechua languages, which originated among the Indigenous people of Peru. Although most Quechua speakers are native to Peru, there are significant populations in Ecuador, Bolivia, Chile, and Argentina.

Quechua creation story

According to our great-great-grandparents, before humans, the realm of Pacha (the cosmos) contained infinite energy called Kallpa. That vital force was the origin of life. Hanac Pacha (heaven) was the heart of the source of life. The essence of life began in the celestial river called Mayu (Milky Way). This divine feature could be seen from the earth with the naked eye. Our ancestors learned how to use their knowledge of Chaskas (stars), paired and grouped in constellations, as a tool to observe the world of the Taytas (gods).

Our Quechua ancestors believed there were three Pachas, with individual Taytas in which they were created. Hanac Pacha was the celestial world in the skies, Kay Pacha was the terrestrial world on Earth, and Uccu Pacha was the spiritual world.

Before human beings came into existence, Kay Pacha, the earth, was occupied by living Taytas. They included Pacha Mama, Apus, plants-Mallkis, rivers-Mayus, winds-Wayras, and animals-Uywas. Hanac Pacha, the celestial Taytas, visible during the day, were the Sun and the Moon. More distant ones, seen clearly at night, included the life giving Mayu (The Milky Way). It had prominent dark blotches, known as Dark Cloud Constellations and contained other geometric forms known as Amaru Machacway (The Serpent), Yuttu (The Tinamou - ground-dwelling birds), Atoq (The Fox), Kuntur (The Condor) and Hamppatu (The Toad).

Taytas were grouped into two categories: luminous stars or constellations. Sparkling stars were arranged in geometric forms named after Taytas. Such as Llama Nawi (The Eye of the Llama), Chacana (Southern Cross), Illary Chaska (Venus), Ccoto (Seven Sisters).

Uccu Paccha was the spiritual world humans could only reach through meditation or personal introspection. Not only the mountains, but all things, had a living spirit and a soul.

Before the birth of humans, Taytas were the only living beings in the Pacha (the cosmos). Taytas were expected to function in harmony with all the gods in all dimensions. But they were banned from wandering between the three dimensions. It was the same as plants and animals can only mate with partners in their own species. Animals can eat plants, but they cannot reproduce new life with them.

Each Tayta was expected to function symbiotically with their partner. Pacha Mama, from Kay Pacha, had to take care of all her brothers and sisters, as the other Taytas were known to each other. Inti, sun, from the Hanac Pacha, provided energy for all the brothers and sisters in Kay Pacha, the planet Earth.

One day, Inti, the sun, constantly collaborating with Pacha mama, entered into a forbidden relationship. The one that was not allowed. But they got to know each other because they always worked together to orchestrate favourable conditions for plants and creatures to flourish, water to flow and winds to blow. Their unthinkable alliance resulted in the birth of the first group of human beings, who began using all the different elements that Pacha Mama provided.

Shamans knew how to use plants like Ayahuasca (Banisteriopsis Caapi - a psychoactive brew) to call the spirits of the mountains as well as the souls of our human ancestors. This awareness of spirit was the foundation of the burial practices of Quechua ancestors. When Quechua people died, their bodies were wrapped and prepared for burial. The mummies were always placed in the foetal position. Because this is the position that humans were in before their birth into Kay Pacha and the most advantageous for the dead person's spirit to be born again. Sacred mummies were protected by placing them on the cliffs. They were vessels of all the accumulated wisdom and knowledge of the person who died. For this reason, they were greatly revered. Quechua people honoured their dead by presenting small gifts to the mummy, a practice that continues today.

Aymara people

The Aymara people are an Indigenous South American group native to the Altiplano region at the lower elevations of the Andes in Argentina, Bolivia, Chile, and Peru. Early Aymara peoples inhabited the same area they live in today continually for more than 5,000 years.

The Creation

Lord Con Ticci Viracocha created Earth and the heavens, as well as the first people.

When they displeased him, he flooded the Earth and started over again. First, he created nature and animals. Then he created humans out of stone and divided them into groups and communities with the help of his companions. He taught them how to live on the land. They lived upon the earth in the darkness of eternal night.

But Lord Con Ticci Viracocha was soon angered by the behaviour of the race and turned them to stone. One group of people emerged armed with rocks... and attacked Viracocha. He punished them by causing fire to fall from the heavens and then created a great flood to wipe out everything.

He then organized the new humans into groups with their own allotted languages, types of food, etc. Viracocha became a human teacher. But when a group attacked him, he taught them a lesson. After his work was done, he and his followers walked across the ocean and withdrew from mankind.

Lord Con Ticci Viracocha set the moon and sun on their paths and used punishment to control humans. Viracocha created people in all phases of life and divided all humans into communities with their own distinct ways of life. He taught people how to live on the land and treat each other with kindness and respect.

Although Viracocha could be kind, he punished those who disturbed the peace in the world, teaching them to obey him.

Viracocha created pregnant women and women first and started the process of caring for the children (in Bolivian culture, men are less important). When Viracocha first created the different groups of humans, he gifted them certain aspects of their cultures, including the songs each group would sing.

People living at Tiahuanaco, awed with Viracocha's power, made a great stone statue of their creator, the all-powerful, all-knowing, and all-perfect god and established a place of worship upon the site.

Tiwanaku. Bolivia

Southern Cone of South America

The earliest evidence for human habitation in South America dates to 14,000 years back in Southern Chile. The Pacific Ocean covers almost one-third of the Earth's surface. Yet, indigenous populations of South America and the Polynesians from the Pacific Islands met 900 years ago, many hundred years before the European colonists arrived in America.

Who met whom we still don't know for sure, but currently scientists favour that Polynesians might have sailed to the Americas. Polynesian navigators, gifted mariners, used the night sky, the sun, birds, clouds, and the reading of ocean swells.

The Yaghan, also called Yagán, Yahgan, Yámana, Yamana or Tequenica, are some of the indigenous peoples of the Southern Cone, regarded as the southernmost peoples in the world. Their traditional territory includes the islands south of Isla Grande de Tierra del Fuego, extending into Cape Horn. Fuegians are one of the three tribes of indigenous inhabitants of Tierra del Fuego, at the southern tip of South America.

First, a story about Fuegia Basket

Uruguayan Jorge Gemetto found a novel, "Fuegia", by Argentine writer Eduardo Belgrano Rawson.The book narrates the adventures of fictional characters. It was dedicated to Fuegia Basket, Jemmy Button, York Minster and Boat Memory. But who was Fuegia Basket? Later, Jorge stumbled upon Darwin's "Voyage of the Beagle" and was surprised when he encountered the character Fuegia Basket.

Darwin wrote in this diary about his first expedition through South America in the 1830s. He describes a nine-year-old girl, Fuegia Basket and three men from Tierra del Fuego kidnapped by his ship HMS Beagle.   Fuegia, Jemmy Button, York Minster and Boat Memory (as the others were called) were taken to England.

After a year in England, during the second expedition of the Beagle, Fuegia, Jemmy Button and York Minster were returned to their land (Boat Memory died of smallpox in England). Darwin highlighted Fuegia's intelligence, charisma, and ability to learn languages: she learned English, Spanish, and Portuguese. Fuegia's birth name was Yokcushlu. Her kidnappers invented her name as Fuegia Basket.

Fuegia Basket (by Henry Colburn)

The English kidnappers had an ulterior motive for returning the Fuegians to their country; they thought that by doing so, the English ships would have an interpreter on future trips through the region.

Despite being abroad for a year, Fuegia refused to join a Christian mission when she reached adulthood. She preferred to share a life linked to their roots and traditions with her family. Fuegia stands out and shines in this painful scenario, but tragically, Fuegia's story is not unique. The kidnapping of Native Americans considered savages by Europeans was typical during the 19th and early 20th centuries. They were often subjected to torments in the name of colonial progress, used as specimens for experimentation or exhibited in human zoos.

In 1889, the pitiful businessman Maurice Maitre took eleven Selk'nam to Paris by force to exhibit them in the human zoos of the (civilised!) World's Fair. Of the 11 people he captured, 2 died on the way there. They were put in cages and given horse meat to eat. A missionary society man protested their condition. He cancelled their tour to England and instead took them to Belgium. Two more died on the way there. In Belgium, they were jailed for being immigrants. Only six finally returned to Tierra del Fuego.

Massacre of the indigenous people by the colonists: Argentinians, Chileans, and British colonists came to the island searching for gold, adventure, or farming land. Frequent harassment, murder, rape of women, invasion of their land and dissipation of their food (Lama) caused the Selk'nam people to retaliate by burning the ranches and killing the sheep for food ('the white guanaco').

The colonist cattle corporations then proceeded to actively exterminate the population by financing killing campaigns. They would pay a pound for each Selk'nam adult and half a pound for each child. The ears, hands, and breasts of women were turned in as proof. Alongside the hunting and massacres of the Selk'nam, the Europeans were responsible for bringing in tuberculosis and smallpox unknown on the continent until then.

Selk'nam People

The Selk'nam, also known as the Ona people, are indigenous in the Patagonian region of southern Argentina and Chile, including the Tierra del Fuego islands. Selk'nam believed all the forms of nature, the atmospheric phenomena, the elements in the sky and the animals were once human beings, transformed into mountains, rivers, animals, etc.

Selk'nam creation story

Temaukel, the Great God, since before the existence of the Earth is the Supreme Being that exists as life exists. Temaukel sent Kenos (an ancestor) to build the world and everything in it. Kenos created the mountains, waterways, and skies. Since there wasn't much light, Kenos created Kreeh and Kreen, the Moon and the Sun. He then asked the Sun to brighten up the sky at noon and leave in the afternoon, to be replaced by the Moon. The sky was very close to the Earth, so Kenos pushed it up.

Kenos grabbed a haruwenthos (a patch of grass mixed with soil), squeezed out the water and planted it back. It formed a Sees (male genital). Then, he grabbed another lump of haruwenthos, created an Asken (female genital) and left it there. At every sunset, the Sees and Asken would join, and a human would be born. The humans would grow and create new humans. After a short time, the land was populated.

Kenos taught the first Selk'nam their language. Kenos got old and tried to start a dream of metamorphosis, a "sleep-death" where you wake up refreshed and young. Since he couldn't succeed, Kenos and three other ancestors began a trek up north. When they got tired of walking, they stopped and asked other ancestors to cover them inside their capes and bury them.

They stayed in a state of "sleep-death" for a long time. When they woke up, they were young again. When the rest of the Selk'nam saw this, they did the same thing. Sometimes they wouldn't wake from their dream of metamorphosis as young again. And this meant that they would transform into hills, animals, waterways.

When it was Kenos's time finally to go, everyone who had stayed with him populated the sky as stars.

Antarctica

Who really discovered Antarctica? Depends on who you ask.

Marinus, an Arabic mathematical geographer from Syria, 2000 years back, coined the term Antarctica, opposite of the Arctic Circle. In the 15th/16th century, the rounding of Cape Horn and Cape of Good hope, southern tips of South America and Africa, respectively, suggested an unknown southern continent. Captain John Davis, an English born American sailor and seal hunter, was the first human landing on Antarctica. Many expeditions attempted to reach the South Pole in the early 20th century. Finally, Norwegian Roald Amundsen reached the pole in December 1911. Caroline Mikkelsen from Denmark was the first woman to step foot onto Antarctica in 1935.

Antarctica is the only continent on Earth without indigenous human inhabitants, despite its proximity to Argentina and Chile on the Antarctic Peninsula.

Drake Passage: The Drake Passage separates South America and Antarctica and connects the Atlantic with the Pacific Ocean. It is 980 km from Tierra del Fuego, the southernmost tip of South America, to any landmass to the south. The Drake Passage joining the Atlantic with the Pacific is considered one of the most treacherous voyages for ships to make. Coupled with the area's propensity for high wind, meeting no resistance from any landmass, it regularly results in waves around 12 meters. Hence its reputation as "the most powerful convergence of seas".

Southern Ocean: The Southern Ocean is the fourth largest ocean in the world, surrounding the entire continent of Antarctica. It has a maximum depth of about 7,300m. It is the conduit through which heat, freshwater, and biogeochemical properties are transported between the Atlantic, Indian, and Pacific Ocean basins.

Playing a vital role in the ventilation of ocean interiors, it is thus a critical part of the global ocean-atmosphere-cryosphere system. This mysterious ocean has absorbed 15% of carbon emissions created by humans so far. It may hold the secret to carbon emission absorption.

Although the Southern Ocean forms a continuous band around the high Southern latitudes, it is not of uniform width. Instead, it is marked by several "choke points". The narrowest of these is the Drake Passage.

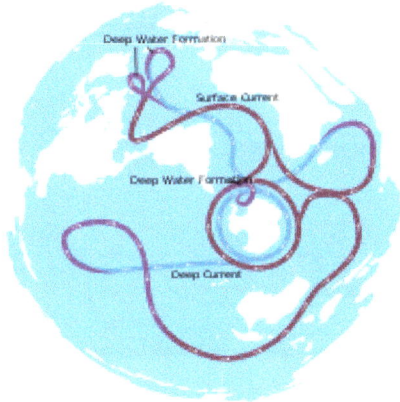

Water circulates around the globe as if it was on a conveyor belt

The Antarctic sea ice cover around Antarctica is highly seasonal, with very little ice between November and February. But in the winter months, it expands to an area roughly equal to Antarctica.

Antarctica is the largest ice store on earth

Antarctica covers 14.2 million km² and is the 5th largest continent. The Antarctic ice sheet is the largest ice store on the planet. On average, its ice sheet is 2,160m thick, with a maximum depth of 4776m, half the height of Mt Everest, making Antarctica the highest continent. 90% of all the world's ice and 70% of all the world's fresh water is in the Antarctic. If all the Antarctic ice sheets melted, the sea level around the world would rise by about 60 meters. The continent is twice the size of Australia, 1.5 times the size of the United States.

Antarctica Interesting Facts

Antarctica is the largest ice store on earth

Antarctica covers 14.2 million km² and is the 5th largest continent. The Antarctic ice sheet is the largest ice store on the planet. On average, its ice sheet is 2,160m thick, with a maximum depth of 4776m, half the height of Mt Everest, making Antarctica the highest continent. 90% of all the world's ice and 70% of all the world's fresh water is in the Antarctic. If all the Antarctic ice sheets melted, the sea level around the world would rise by about 60 meters. The continent is twice the size of Australia, 1.5 times the size of the United States.

There is no time zone.

Whichever you look, every direction is north at the South Pole

There is no Antarctic time zone. At the South Pole, the lines of longitude, which give us different time zones around the globe, all meet at a single point. If you stand at the South Pole, you are at the southernmost point on Earth. Whichever way you look, every direction is north. Precisely the opposite happens at the other end of our planet on the North Pole. Most of Antarctica experiences 6 months of constant daylight in summer and 6 months of darkness in winter. Scientists working in Antarctica generally use the time zone of their own country.

Antarctica was once a rainforest

The lowest surface temperature on Earth ever recorded was -98 °C (-144 °F) in Antarctica. But Antarctica once used to be warm and temperate. Around 40-50 million years ago, temperatures across Antarctica were up to 17°C. Fossils have been found showing that Antarctica was once covered with verdant green forests and inhabited by dinosaurs!

Approximately 200 million years ago, Antarctica belonged to a supercontinent called Gondwana, including Australia, Africa, India, and South America. Here, many thousands of species of plants flourished for many millions of years. As the continents began to split away from each other around 145-66 million years ago, Antarctica drifted towards the South Pole. Most plants were able to survive and continued to grow during the continental movement. Soon, the climate became much too cold, dry and unsuitable for sustaining most life forms. Fossilized remains of tropical trees and leaf impressions suggest once green and lush Antarctic rainforests.

There are now only two flowering plants in Antarctica

There are no trees or shrubs now in Antarctica, only two flowering plants: Antarctic hair grass (Deschampsia Antarctica) and Antarctic pearlwort (Colobanthus quitensis). But there are over 1000 species of fungi, 700 species of algae and 20-odd species of macro-fungi. There are also around 100 species of mosses, 25 species of liverworts, and 300 to 400 species of lichens in Antarctica. And living in these micro-forests are 67 species of insects!

Unusual creatures

Antarctica is a barren, icy desert with very little rain, fierce winds, and the coldest temperatures on earth, yet it's also home to a myriad of unique wildlife. Several unusual species have adapted to this harsh environment. There are microbes, crustaceans, colossal squid, leggy spiders the size of dinner plates, giant worms with shiny golden bristles and a large, sharp-toothed jaw. Some of these creatures here have antifreeze glycoproteins and cannot survive in warmer waters.

Many fossils have been found from marine animals, birds and dinosaurs from the Cretaceous Period and forewings of a beetle species that lived between 14 and 20 million years ago in a warmer climate. Extraordinarily, fifty-million-year old sperm cells on the egg case of a long-extinct worm species have been discovered in Antarctica. The scientists hope this will lead to new evolutionary information.

Antarctica is now home to many animal species

Antarctica is home to hundreds of different animal species, including 46 species of bird, 10 cetaceans (including killer whales and humpback whales, 6 species of seal and 7 Antarctic penguin species. There are also at least 235 species in Antarctica's oceans, from mud-dwelling worms to sea cucumbers, sea snails and sea birds.

The Antarctic sponge holds the record for the longevity of its kind. They live at a depth of about 200m, where sunlight does not reach. By reducing their metabolic process, the Antarctic sponge can live up to 15,000 years!

Humans now live, and babies have been born in Antarctica

The Antarctic Treaty of 1959 was initially signed by 12 countries, which blocked any nation from taking over this winter wonderland. Since then, 41 other countries have signed the Treaty. It now includes strict guidelines for commercial fishing, sealing, and a complete mining and mineral exploration ban.

But Argentina and Chile, even after signing the treaty, continue to claim that the Antarctic Peninsula is a continuation of the Andes Mountains. This is mainly because of the reserves of coal, oil and an unknown quantity of other minerals. However, mining and extracting coal and oil is currently illegal.

In 1977 Argentina sent a pregnant woman to Antarctica to claim partial possession of the continent. On January 7, 1978, Silvia Morello de Palma was the first woman in history to give birth on the continent. Emilio Palma was the first person to be born in Antarctica. After his birth, the Argentine government passed a law to include Antarctica within all maps of the country! Chile played along. Absurdly they sent a few recently married couples to their Antarctic base to claim the first baby both conceived and born in Antarctica. Altogether eleven children had been born in Antarctica, eight at the Argentinian Base and the other three at Chile's Base.

At present, about 4,000 scientists from 30 countries live on about 70 bases (40 year-round and 30 summer-only) during the summer months in the Antarctic. But in the winter, there are only around 1000 in all the bases combined. But the longest time spent on the continent by anyone is 15 months (two summers and one winter).

Antarctica is a desert

Antarctica is a desert, the highest, driest, coldest and windiest continent on Earth. The driest place on Earth is in the Dry Valleys of Antarctica, which have seen no rain for nearly 2 million years. The average annual rainfall at the South Pole over the past 30 years was just only 10mm. Antarctica may be covered in ice now, but it has taken an incredible 45 million years to grow to its current thickness because of so little rainfalls.

Diamonds floating in the air

One of the meteorological wonders in Antarctica includes diamond dust. Diamond dust is made of tiny ice crystals, like an icy fog near the Earth's surface. Hanging Ice crystals in the air sparkle in the sunlight, creating a glittering effect, looking like a million tiny floating diamonds.

Blood Falls

Antarctica has a subglacial lake flowing blood red. In the McMurdo Dry Valley, a bright crimson five-storey waterfall pours out of Taylor Glacier into

Lake Bonney. It looks like a gush of blood from a wound in the ice. The lily-white ice of the Taylor Glacier is stained a deep red by water high in salt and oxidised iron flowing from deep. When this water meets, oxygen rusts the iron, hence its name Blood Falls.

Singing ice

A massive slab of ice in Antarctica is singing. The Ross Ice, the largest ice shelf in Antarctica, covers over 500,000 Sq Km. The Ross Ice Shelf sings eerie melody caused by the winds blowing across the snow dunes. The mournful tune is not audible to human ears, only by seismic sensors. The song changes in response to the environment, such as melting or storms shifting the snow. The song is now used as a tool to monitor the ice shelf, tracking its stability and vulnerability for collapse.

Ancient meteorites

Antarctica is a goldfield for meteorites. Although meteorites can fall all over the earth, they are easier to find in Antarctica as the cold, dry conditions preserve the rocky fragments. The dark meteorites are also easier to spot on the stark white surface of the ice. More than 20,000 extra-terrestrial meteorite samples have been collected there since 1976, including an incredible 18 kg rock. The discoveries included a piece of the asteroid Vesta, the second most massive body in the asteroid belt, and meteorites from Mars.

Sundog

A sundog is a bright, rainbow-coloured patch of light occurring on either side of the sun when it is low on the horizon, during sunrise or sunset. Sometimes, a pair of sundogs may appear, one on the sun's left and another on its right.

Sundogs form when sunlight is refracted (bent) by ice crystals suspended in the atmosphere. This phenomenon is related to atmospheric halos, which are white and coloured rings in the sky that form by the same process. These optical events "sit" beside the sun, like a loyal dog attends its owner, hence the name sundog.

Underground lakes

It's difficult to imagine anything beneath Antarctica's thick layers of ice, but around 400 lakes sit here under 3km of ice. The lakes don't freeze because of the pressure from the weight of the ice sheet. More interestingly, in 2014, scientists discovered a diverse and active eco-system of microorganisms in the lake, nearly 1 km under the ice sheet. These incredible species haven't seen fresh air or sunlight for millions of years. Yet, they flourish, using methane and ammonium as energy to grow.

There are many Volcanoes

It is hard to believe, but deep ice-covered Antarctica is home to several volcanoes, two of which are active. Mount Erebus, the second-highest volcano in Antarctica, is the southernmost active volcano on Earth.

Mt Erebus

Climate change

But ice-covered Antarctica is now one of the most rapidly warming areas on Earth. In the past 50 years, average temperatures across the Antarctic have increased by 3°C, five times the average increase on Earth. The high ice sheet and the polar location make Antarctica a powerful global heat sink. This strongly affects the climate of the whole Earth. Furthermore, the annual sea ice cover around the continent, which in winter reaches an area larger than that of the continent itself, modulates exchanges of heat, moisture, and gases between the atmosphere and ocean. Alterations to this system will significantly affect climate all over the planet.

Antarctic species are dramatically impacted by climate as well. Krill that feed on algae underneath sea ice is declining in population as the Antarctic sea ice decreases. Adélie penguin populations have been declining due to reductions in krill populations and changing weather conditions in their traditional nesting areas. Emperor penguins are also highly vulnerable and are predicted to suffer soon.

Climate change in Antarctica will thus have dramatic effects both globally and locally - and harm some of the world's most beloved species.

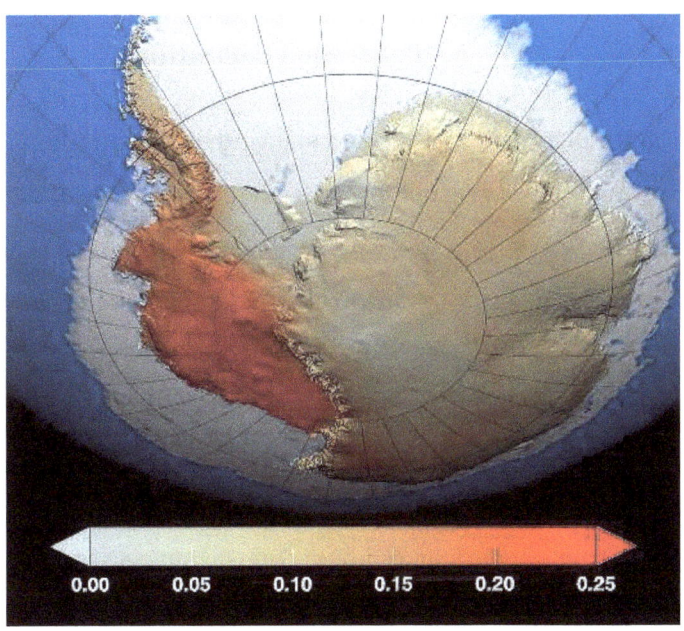

Acknowledgement

I would like to thank scientists and scientific journals worldwide for the materials in my book. I am also grateful to researchers and collectors of ancient stories from all the continents for my collection. I am grateful for these and hope they will give our young readers a glimpse into our wonderful world and encourage them to respect and explore more.

I am indebted to everyday people from all the continents I have visited, inspiring me to look at our world more respectfully. Hopefully, some of their wisdom and care for nature will be passed on to the future generation.

Finally, I would like to acknowledge Julius Apelanio (Master Jo) and 99designs for their help with the book cover and IngramSpark for their help in publishing this book and opening it to the next generation.

Illustration dedications

I am grateful to the following and many other websites for the images used in this book, which will give our young readers a wide view of our wonderful planet : en wikipedia.org, geeky.news, Alex Miltomann/Cold creation, space.com, Khan Academy, ucl.ac.uk, guyhowto.com, newscientist.com, wordpress.com, nhm.ac.uk, researchgate.net, afktravel.com, hiiibrand.com, africasafarimagazine.com, beyonder.travel, everyevery.ng; ancient-egypt-online.com, History.com, asianage.com, twitter.com, shine.cn, papuanewguinea.travel, Decan Herald, mauikayakadventures.com, bavipower.com, geneticlitearcyproject.com, mythologysource.com, gsfc.nasa.gov, the-past.com, legendsofamerica.com, oneidaindiannation.com, navajopeople.org, thoughtco.com, revuemag.com, worldatlas.com, wikiwand.com, bas.ac.uk, mpora.com, earthobservatory.nasa.gov.

About the author

Born in Joteram village in West Bengal, India, Biku Ghosh OBE worked in the UK as a specialist surgeon for over forty years and now lives in Ivybridge, Devon, UK. Apart from travelling to over seventy-five countries on all seven continents, he has worked as a volunteer in twelve countries on five continents.

His travel memoir 'Around the world in 65 years' was published in 2020. His other book, 'Indian Immigrant', a historical fiction, about how colonialism powerfully altered what being '*Indian*' meant culturally and legally in Britain, was published in 2018.

Email- Bikughosh@gmail.com

Facebook – biku.ghosh.75   Twitter - @GhoshBiku

Instagram – bikughosh7 and bookbiku

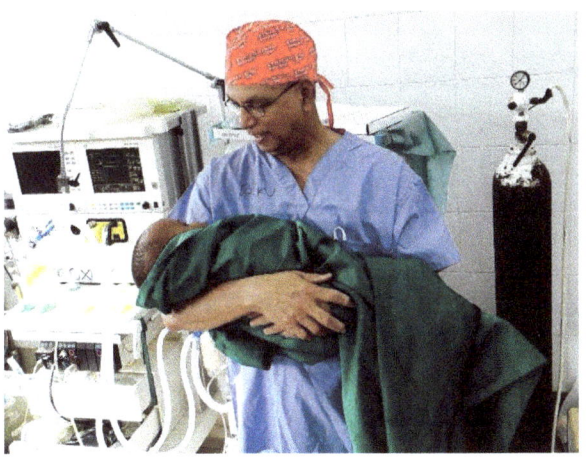

9 781838 191788